JEWS WITHOUT MERCY
A LAMENT

JEWS
WITHOUT
MERCY

A Lament

By Earl Shorris

1982   Anchor Press/Doubleday, Garden City, New York

Chapter 9 originally appeared, in a different form, in the *Antioch Review*, and later appeared in *The Bar Mitzvah Book*, published in the United States by Praeger Publishers.

Library of Congress Cataloging in Publication Data

Shorris, Earl, 1936–
Jews without mercy.

1. Jews—United States—Politics and government.
2. Judaism and social problems.   3. Right and left
(Political science)   4. United States—Politics and
government—1945–   . I. Title.
E184.J5S484   973'.04924
AACR2
ISBN 0-385-17853-0

In memory of my father, who opposed communism,
fascism, and the New York Yankees;
who took up the politics of mercy
in his youth and never wavered

FOREWORD

No one speaks for the Jews. We are the people of the great fraction; the whole of us must always be described as the number of Jews divided by the number of Jews. Even Moses was permitted no role greater than that of messenger. We are a nation by belief, by ethics, and by history. We are difficult to lead, impossible to collect, a tribe of individuals, a brotherhood of critics.

From time to time in our history men and women have come forward claiming to speak as Jews for Jews. The temptation to proclaim oneself king or prophet in a nation of equals before God is enormous, for God does not seem to answer many prayers. Jews are not likely to turn away the self-proclaimed king or prophet without a hearing, for the life of a Jew offers little ease: History holds little promise, heaven remains in dispute; we are not hostages to fortune but to ethics.

The Law is not a law of solace. So unforgiving are the rabbis in their exegesis of Jewish ethics that they demand the coming of a messianic period prior to the coming of a messiah; in other words, we can only be saved by saving ourselves. It is a difficult life. We are intolerant of fools, but we never fail to give them a hearing. We despise schemes for ease that would destroy our ethical definition of ourselves, but we would like to get off the hook.

As each new challenge to our ethical existence arises, a chorus of Jewish voices answers. The current challenge comes from within the ranks of Jews. A group of men and women claiming to be both Jews and neoconservatives now proposes that Jews accept a new ethical definition of themselves, a definition contrary to much, perhaps most, of what has defined us since our historical beginning in the desert after we were sojourners in Egypt.

This book seeks to answer that proposal. It is but one voice. More eloquent and more learned voices will also answer.

I did not want to write this book. It is a homely little book, with no intention but to raise some arguments at the kitchen table or to trigger a thought or two on the way to the office or the theater. I am obliged to write it because I have (except for a few comic moments) always been pleased to be a Jew. The gift deserves to be defended.

If too much of my own life appears in this book, I ask your indulgence. It could as well have been your life as mine: Every life has stories in it; every life is a connection between ethics and the world; all of us have a history. The Law belongs to all of us, too, and we are told to think about it as best we can, which is all that I have done.

Yet, you must ask, as I have: How can a man of little piety, virtually no learning, and uncertain ethics presume to write a book such as this? If the neoconservatives cannot speak for Jews, how can I? The answer is that this is an answer; if they had not said the ethics of my fathers were wrong, I would not be compelled to defend those ethics.

Finally, there is the question of whether a book like this

should be written by a common man, one who works in the world, a man unlike the Jewish neoconservatives, who live by grants and fellowships and the security of tenure. Akiva and Hillel worked in the world, Rashi was a vintner, Maimonides was a physician; an ordinary businessman can at least take refuge in these lines from the end of an argument in the Talmud: "He who has neither learnt nor taught, neither kept nor done, Torah, but who, having the opportunity to encourage and abet others, availed himself of it, is blessed."

ACKNOWLEDGMENTS

A cool, detailed, and brilliantly analytical book, *The Neo-Conservatives* by Peter Steinfels is, I believe, the indispensable work on the neoconservative movement. It is also a good antidote for the very personal view put forward in this book. An excellent review of the history of *Commentary* and its hard turn to the right appeared in the spring 1981 issue of *Dissent;* in that brief essay Bernard Avishai provides a thoughtful counterweight to Norman Podhoretz's autobiographical polemics. Both works have been helpful to me, and I am certain that anyone interested in the neoconservative movement will find them useful and interesting.

This is not an easy book to publish, either for the writer or the publisher. To all the kind people who advised me against writing this book for fear of the power of the neoconservatives to make life difficult for me and my work, and to all the people who said that others would think the title of this book anti-Semitic, although they were too wise to think it so, I am not at all grateful.

Fortunately, I do not count many timid people among my friends. Some of them may disagree with what is written here, but they encouraged the writing anyway. I am grateful to these friendly champions of contentiousness: A. M. Ducovny, Lewis H. Lapham, Mitchel Levitas, Leo Litwak, Philip and Elizabeth Pochoda, Marcella Rosen, Charles Simmons, and Matthew Stevenson. Rabbi Leo Jung was kind enough to read the manuscript and comment on it. Would that a man as learned as he had written it!

I also wish to thank my friend and literary agent, John Ware, for his steadfast support of my work. This book might not have been published were it not for the indomitable Loretta Barrett, and it would surely have been even more riddled with lapses of thought and taste if she and Paul Aron had not read so carefully or thought so clearly.

The burden of writing books belongs as much to my wife as to me; whatever good comes of them is also hers.

CONTENTS

It hath been told thee, O man, what is good;
And what the Lord doth require of thee;
Only to do justly, and to love mercy,
And to walk humbly with thy God.

MIC. 6:8

Leopards break into the temple and drink to the dregs what is in the sacrificial pitchers; this is repeated over and over again; finally it can be calculated in advance, and it becomes a part of the ceremony.

FRANZ KAFKA

JEWS WITHOUT MERCY
A LAMENT

1. Apology to Mr. Singer, Slayer of Chickens, May He Rest in Peace

You were decorated with blood and feathers, praying and killing in the back room of a store on an empty block in a failed section of the town. The butcher pointed to you as if you were an advertisement. He asked if the boy wanted to watch Mr. Singer do his work. I declined to step behind the counter and through the unpainted wooden gate that led to your slaughterhouse. My grandmother laughed. She knew chickens, she knew children.

She prepared chickens in the tiny kitchen of her apartment, reaching into the hollow cavity to remove the liver, heart, and kidneys; tearing the fat from the flesh; and depositing the yellow clumps in a saucepan. She burned the feet in the fire of the stove, blackening the ends of the truncated toes. While the chicken soaked in salt water she spoke of you: You dassn't be afraid of Mr. Singer. He's a very learned man. When the Rabbi has a question, you know where he goes? To Mr. Singer!

Nevertheless, I did not go again with my grandmother to the chicken store, preferring to spend summer afternoons in her care, lying on a couch, drinking strawberry soda, and listening to the baseball game. But I watched you; on the Sabbath, on holy days I watched you. The rabbi, the president of the congregation, and the cantor sat facing the congregation, but you were always the first one called up from among us to join them; the first honor always went to you. In the puddle of old men who remained in the synagogue during the hot afternoon doldrums of Yom Kippur, two yarmulkes stood out among the sweated fedoras, yours and mine. One tallith was more venerable, truer than the rest, the great yellowed black-and-white shawl that covered your back and shoulders.

When we stood to recite our sins, I saw the old men in their gray suits—their faces garnished with white stubble and their words roaring on the sour breath of the last hours of the fast—strike their chests in time to the chanting of the litany. You did not strike your chest, nor were your words a roaring to God. You prayed as if the sins of the congregation were also your sins. You told me by the sincerity of your voice that we were a nation; you explained the meaning of community.

It was not until I began to come to minyans that you spoke to me. You pointed to the place in the English text. I pointed to the place in the Hebrew text.

You read Hebrew?

A little.

You put on tefillin?

Yes.

You know what it means putting on tefillin?

I'm learning.

You closed your eyes, pursed your lips, and nodded. You asked my name.

Earl.

I was used to a boy's name, to hearing old men respond to my name with the name of my father and my grandfather, but you said, That's not a name.

Yehuda.

You know what this means?

Judah. I'm Judah the son of Samuel.

No. Yehuda means a Jew. This is a name to think about.

The man in front of us turned around and put his finger to his lips, and you answered, perhaps to him, perhaps to me, In the Ḥumash we are told first to learn the laws, then to keep them.

That night I stayed awake, reading through the Pentateuch until I found the place where study came before action. It was there, at the beginning of Chapter Five of Deuteronomy, the Book of Words, just as you had said. I vowed to become a rabbi.

We spoke once more that summer. You asked, What will you be when you grow up? A doctor?

A rabbi, said the boy who put on tefillin in the morning and read the Bible at night, who continued to go to ḥeder after he was bar mitzvah, who taught children of his own age in the Sunday School.

Yehuda, you said, to be a good Jew it's not necessary to be a rabbi.

The next time I saw you was Erev Yom Kippur. We arrived at the synagogue as a family, three generations led by my grandfather. There were ritual greetings, a crowd on the sidewalk in front of the synagogue, a whole community in its autumn finery, as if God were to inscribe them in the Book of Life according to their dress. The meal before the

fast had been eaten, the old men smoked their last cigarettes, and the children beginning their first fast had a last
sip of water before sundown.

My grandfather spoke to his friend Eddie—Big Eddie he
called him. They spoke as members of the board of directors
of the synagogue, important men, big donors. My grandfather earned his money from the labor of Italian and Polish
women who sewed clothing in his factories. Big Eddie sold
cheap wine and whiskey to the poor of the town. We did
not approve of Big Eddie. His diamond ring and his fat
cigar offended us, his penchant for reddish-brown suits that
matched his curly hair offended us, his business offended us.
There were fights in front of his store, stabbings, more than
one killing. There were rumors about him. Some people said
he dealt with criminals. It was said that he gave so much to
the synagogue to atone for the way he made his money.

No one shunned Big Eddie; he would not permit it. He
overwhelmed people with greetings, he grabbed at hands,
he took shoulders, he surrounded people in cigar smoke.
Nor could the official community shun him: He traded do-
nations for a position as a director of the synagogue. My
grandfather said Eddie wanted to be president, that he was
willing to donate a community center if the directors would
elect him president.

Perhaps you knew all of this, perhaps piety and politics
mixed easily in you. It didn't matter. You found out soon
enough. I watched from the first row of the balcony as you
learned.

It was the only time of the year when the entire congregation came to the synagogue. Every seat in every pew was
filled. Young people and visitors and newcomers were
ushered upstairs to the balcony for the singing of Kol Nidre.
It was to be your night, as it had always been, the night of
the recognition of piety, the good night.

From my perch in the balcony the congregation was a

garden of hats: The fedoras were the leaves, the women's
hats the flowers. It was a somber autumn garden. Your
black yarmulke was like an old seed left over from another
season. I watched you remove your tallith from its velvet
case. You kissed it twice, you covered your head, and then
you let the yellowed fabric ease down over your back and
shoulders.

You sat on the aisle, close to the front. You were not
proud, you were not beaming, as a less pious man might
have been. I wondered what you were thinking, if it was
like your bar mitzvah. You rose to shake hands with the
rabbi, with the president of the congregation, and with the
cantor. I knew what you were saying. It was not banter
about business or the weather. You forgave them for any
sins they might have committed against you. They gave you
their forgiveness in return. It was the last opportunity before sundown.

The rabbi stepped up to the pulpit, the people in the
pews righted themselves and fell silent. The service began.
In a moment or two the first aliyah would be given. All that
was worldly in the congregation would be atoned for in the
recognition of the learned one, the old man Singer, who
loved God and all of His laws. The reward for good and evil
is here on earth.

We saw the president of the congregation go to the other
side of the bimah. We watched him intently, you and I, and
I wondered even in that moment if you had known when
you forgave him. It was wrong, it was all going wrong; the
Jews were becoming a caricature of Jews. And it was hap-
pening in God's house on the eve of the day of the writing
of our names in the Book of Life.

I did not begin to cry until Big Eddie stood up, so red in
that somber garden, shaking the hands of the men around
him, while the beadle of our synagogue stood in the aisle at
the end of Big Eddie's pew holding a tallith for him. Big

Eddie took the tallith as if it were a scarf, looping it around his neck. He said no blessing, he did not kiss the beginning and the end of the embroidered words, he did not cover his head. He strode down the aisle to take his prize, running up the five steps to the bimah with the aggressive bounce of a nightclub singer beginning his show.

You waited for the president to cross the platform to your side to offer the second aliyah to you. I hoped you would decline the honor, but you rose as always and walked slowly up the steps to the platform. The second Torah was taken from the Ark and put in your arms. You were its old lover, its frail defender. You stood beside Big Eddie. I could not read your eyes from my place in the balcony. He laughed. The color of his flesh was as rich and vulgar as his suit. You were so small, so pale beside him. Jerusalem was conquered, the Temple was destroyed, and there was no prophet in all of Israel.

After the service I asked my father why it had happened. Money, was all he said.

Sometimes you have to do these things, my grandfather added. A building doesn't come cheap.

That night I lay on the bed in my room, hot and thirsty, waiting for some autumn wind to cool me. I looked in the Bible for an explanation. Only Ecclesiastes spoke to me, and that unhappy schoolmaster offered no solace. I knew that the breeze I waited for would be an empty breath. I understood the meaning of vanity.

Sometime after midnight I went downstairs to the kitchen and poured cold water into a glass. You told me not to drink the water, Mr. Singer, but your words had become vanity. I drank the water as if it were poison. Then I ate cookies, a peach, bread, meat, lettuce, and a lump of butter. I tasted sugar, salt, pepper, and spice. I even put a drop of vinegar on my tongue. When I went upstairs to my room it was cooler. The curtains moved. I straightened my bed and lay down on my back, arranging my body neatly, as if my limbs were things. Then I closed my eyes and waited to die.

You knew I would not become a rabbi, but you were too kind to say so. How did you think the failure would come? Was it a lack of faith? sloth? the comforts of assimilation? Did the apotheosis of things merely serve as an excuse?

Mr. Singer, at one o'clock in the afternoon of that Yom Kippur my father also broke the fast. It was the first time food or drink had passed his lips on Yom Kippur in more than thirty years. He did not leave Judaism. Every morning and every evening for all the rest of his life he prayed, but no one spoke to God on his behalf since that Yom Kippur, no one determined for him who should be honored.

Did you continue to fast? Did you continue to come to minyans so that impious men might mumble the kaddish without knowing that they prayed for themselves? What did you say to the chickens?

If you had raised your voice in protest, would it have been an act of piety or would you have pulled our small-town temple down into the chaos of the unenlightened East? If only you had danced with rage, twirling a chicken round your head! Instead you were so meek in your righteousness that hardly anyone in the congregation noticed the injustice that evening.

Now I am older than my father was on the night Big Eddie became the man our community commended to God, and you are long dead. You did not live to force many more young men to question the reward for righteousness. Why were you silent? Did you mean to leave this work to me? Did you mean for all of us to be silent so that the buildings might be built? Shall we study ethics in whispers and die before we are made to witness the second destruction of the Temple?

You were meek for the good of the Jews. That is what you said when you said nothing and died. But every morning of your life you said The Thirteen Principles of Faith. What did you mean when you said, "I believe with perfect faith that all the words of the prophets are true?" Should they have been silent for the good of the Jews?

Something has gone wrong in the world you left behind. Big Eddie has created a faction of Jews without mercy, and Jews without mercy are not Jews, although they claim to speak for our "interests." No more lamentable thing has happened to us since you died, Mr. Singer. If we do not dispute them, what will we become?

Forgive me for speaking, Mr. Singer. I do not want to die.

Forgive me if I now speak bluntly, harshly, sometimes in anger. The descendants of Big Eddie, the Jewish neoconservatives, are not gentle people. They are not direct in the way that you were direct with me. Nor do they reason as Jews have been taught to do. Neoconservatism is brutal, often deceptive. One wants to argue with them, but what is the argument against a declaration other than to declare that it is wrong?

They surprised me, as they would have surprised you. We looked once and saw a handful of teachers and writers saying the gentle things one expects of bookish people, saying all the merciful things that are thought to grow in the serenity of universities, teaching ethics to those of us who struggle in the harsh world of chickens and commerce. We looked again and saw the handful at the head of a tweedy mob. Their voices have not changed, they still use the language of the academy and the tone of discourse common among educated men, but they speak the most egregious ideas, they make such terrible sadness in us.

If I listen to them and hear the music of their voices—and

only the music—I begin to think that these teachers are teachers of the truth. It is easy to become the victim of the printed word, the prestigious foundation, the academic degree, the past glory, the language of thinking.

Yes, yes, of course, the best way to help the poor is to take from the poor and give to the rich, for it is only through the creation of riches that the poor will cease to be poor. Did God not say He loved the poor?

Eristic was a game to the Greeks. The Hebrews were not so playful. I cannot be amused by the camouflage of neoconservative argument, for I lack the tradition of playfulness. It seems right to me to dispense with the nets and leaves and to say the tenets of neoconservatism nakedly, the better to examine them.

Is that right and decent? Should there be no place for compromise? Should one not be merciful in arguing for mercy?

You, who never spared a chicken, would not ask me to spare a fox.

And what of forgiveness? you ask. Let the poor forgive them, let the hungry include them in their prayers. Who am I? And if they succeed in fomenting war, let the dead form a choir in heaven to sing forgiveness for them. I will, no doubt, be among the dead. I can wait.

In all the history that you knew, in the narrower history that I know there has never been a time when it was more confusing to be a Jew. How is it that we did not come like saints from the fires? Why are we not all beautiful? Is there no end to the testing?

Most of us came late to America. We were so poor. We had lived so near the bottom, and the dream turned out to be the bottom again. It took us a moment in the counting of history to become Americans, to learn to understand the na-

tion as the community. Strangers could not welcome
strangers; we needed the moment. But even as we ceased to
be strangers we took in strangers; even before we had fields
we shared the corners of the corners of the field.

Socialism, the union movement, the Democratic party,
the social worker, the schoolteacher, liberalism, the welfare
state, the civil rights movement; when some of us became
rich we did not cease to argue for the redistribution of
riches.

The Law spoke for us then. We were a whole culture, we
could remember. Who are these people who claim to speak
for us now? Who are these powerful and frightened people?
What made them so arrogant?

Forgive my anger, Mr. Singer. Silence would be more unseemly now.

The neoconservative Jews have not codified their views.
They are still best identified by the half dozen middle-aged
former leftists who led the garrulous conversion. Norman
Podhoretz, the first to announce that power is an antidote to
vulgarity, writes the doctrine best, clearly and in a style
that seems less and less that of a man who learned English
late in life. Daniel Bell flirts with neoconservatism; much of
it pleases him, but he cannot bring himself to abandon his
commitment to mercy. Irving Kristol, the first to accept the
neoconservative label, has become the jackal of the movement, the last man to support the war in Vietnam and the
first Jew to defend the military governors of Argentina
against charges of anti-Semitism. Nathan Glazer, the chief
neoconservative theoretician in the fight against affirmative
action programs, led in the argument that what is good for
the blacks is no longer good for the Jews. Midge Decter
Podhoretz writes the cruelest prose in defense of the family,
attacking the counterculture, the women's movement, and
homosexuals. Sidney Hook thought he saw Stalin among the

raucous, fearful child rebels of the sixties who called themselves revolutionaries while taking comfort in the knowledge that the revolution would not come and the monthly
allowances from their parents would not stop coming.

The neoconservatives were gentle people, highly educated
but naive academicians. To one who lives in the world of
private business they seem like children who cannot quite
understand what daddy does for a living. Yet they enjoy
money, as Norman Podhoretz has so loudly said. They are
unashamedly ambitious, almost greedy. They do not know
or wish to know the risks of daily life in the world of business; they are more comfortable in the role of consultant,
advising others on which risks to take.

All of them suffer a confusion of geography. Tied to
Europe and European New York, they cannot quite imagine America. They know the history, they have the most recent statistics at hand, but they have no conception of
space, of the way prairies diffuse politics even in the elec-
tronic age, of the interruption a mountain causes to a collective. The miracle of American orneriness that did not show
itself to Toqueville does not show itself to them, for they,
too, are visitors in a new land, differing from Toqueville
only in that their travels are more limited.

They do not always agree with each other about every
issue, but the young seem to follow their older brethren; the
only maverick among them now is Daniel Bell. The rules of
neoconservatism change from time to time, moving slowly
past the political center and on to the right, enjoying a flir-
tation with the Reagan administration. If there are any
clearly defined tenets of neoconservatism, they are:

Capitalism is good for the Jews. Irving Kristol, unsatisfied
with a return to the economics of Adam Smith, has urged
his readers to return to the philosophy of John Calvin.

Jews have escaped their origins and now enjoy the plea-
sures of economic security and even of affluence. Therefore

Jewish interests have changed; Jews should now hold on to what they have. If the blacks, Hispanics, and other groups of poor people wish to escape their origins, they must do so on their own merits; society is not responsible for correcting past injustices by giving more than equal opportunity to the inheritors of injustice.

Affirmative action programs are not similar to quota systems, they *are* quota systems. Quota systems will cause Jews to have to give up their places to blacks, Hispanics, and other disadvantaged people, including women.

Social welfare programs drain the national economy, create wasteful bureaucracies, and destroy the entrepreneurial spirit in recipients of social welfare. A large, although unspecified, percentage of those receiving social welfare are cheating.

The trickle-down theory of the spread of wealth will work in America. Therefore cutting taxes for the rich will do more to aid the poor than will the redistribution of wealth through a highly graduated system of taxation on earnings and other income, inheritances, and even wealth itself.

Egalitarianism leads to left totalitarianism, always has and always will. The drive for egalitarianism, according to Mr. Kristol, is somehow caused by a lack of religious belief.

Equality of opportunity is true justice; equality of outcome is unfair, unjust, morally debilitating, and must ultimately lead to the totalitarian horrors of atheistic communism.

Religion is good for the Jews. If all Americans were religious, bourgeois society would be guaranteed and Jews would be safe.

Blacks betrayed the Jews, the very people who helped them up out of racism and poverty into their current situation. Blacks are anti-Semitic. Jews should not help blacks anymore, nor should they help other minorities, such as

Hispanics, because they will only turn on the Jews as the blacks did.

Regulation of business is wasteful and inhibits the growth of the economy.

Environmentalists and conservationists hurt the growth of the economy for no good reason.

Alger Hiss was guilty.

The Rosenbergs were guilty.

Fidel Castro was and always will be guilty.

The House Committee on Un-American Activities was not so bad as some have said. And neither was Senator Joseph McCarthy, even though both his character and his methods were questionable.

The Hollywood Ten were guilty and the friendly witnesses were the true friends of America.

All those who opposed the Vietnam War are guilty; we should have won the war.

Censorship of sexually explicit material is beneficial to society.

The CIA must be unleashed.

The FBI must be unleashed.

Crime can be stopped if America will only stop coddling criminals.

Capital punishment deters crime.

Moral Majority is not anti-Semitic. Jerry Falwell loves Israel. Many other values put forward by Moral Majority are good for society.

Psychological testing of blacks, indicating the entire race may be inferior, cannot be dismissed out of hand.

A change of cultural values is destroying America, which must return to the traditional values of religion, family, hard work, heterosexuality, male dominance, and puritanical sexual mores.

A new class or adversary class, composed of intellectuals, journalists, government employees, professors, teachers, re-

searchers, various professionals, and even some members of
the clergy, but not including any members of the same oc-
cupational groups who have seen the light of neoconservatism, is responsible for the political, social, economic, and
cultural decline of America.

Russian political dissidents, whether Jews or Gentiles, are
admirably suited, upon arriving in America, to advise Americans on political, social, economic, and cultural matters.

The State of Israel can do no wrong.

The Palestinian people have no right to exist as a state,
nor do Palestinian territorial claims have any validity.

The killing of an Israeli civilian by a Palestinian is an act
of terrorism.

The killing of a Palestinian civilian by an Israeli is a
justifiable act of self-defense.

Occupation and colonization of foreign territory by Israel
is not imperialism.*

Any political position taken by an American Jew is
justified if it can be associated with the survival of Israel.

Any political position taken by an American Jew is
justified if it can be associated with protecting Soviet Jews,
particularly their ability to emigrate.

Communism is a monolithic force in the process of con-
quering the world through craftiness, subversion, military
force, amorality, and collectivistic single-mindedness.

---

* As this book goes to press Israel has annexed the Golan Heights.
The annexation has been declared null and void by the United Nations. The Reagan administration has abrogated a strategic coopera-
tion accord with Israel to show its displeasure with the sudden annexation. Israeli Defense Minister Ariel Sharon has told the press that
the U.S. response damages the security of Israel. The Syrian government, as if to underscore General Sharon's contention, has applauded
the U.S. response.

Thus far, there has been no response from the leaders of the Jewish
neoconservative movement. As supporters of both Mr. Reagan and
Mr. Begin, they have been put in an unenviable position.

Communism is not good for the Jews.

The mob, which is created by communism or leads to communism, is not good for the Jews.

All socialist regimes are anti-Semitic.

The alternative to the mob is a return to traditional cultural values. These values are opposed by the New Left, including McGovern liberals. The left in America therefore foments mob rule, which in turn leads to left totalitarian government, which is bad for the Jews.

The Soviet Union leads the United States in the arms race and seeks to bring America to its knees through the threat of a first strike with superior nuclear forces.

A vast buildup of American arms is the only way to deter the Soviet coup, save Israel, and permit the right-wing dictatorships of the free world to move peacefully along the route to human rights, republican democracy, and economic stability.

Only left-wing regimes can be totalitarian; right-wing regimes are authoritarian.

Jacobo Timerman was guilty of crimes he was not charged with by the Argentine military government.

Israel's export of arms to Argentina, like its export of arms to South Africa, is justified by the need for survival of the State of Israel.

The Likkud party of Israel is okay.

Henry Kissinger may or may not be okay.

Richard Nixon was okay and may be okay again someday.

Senator Henry Jackson should have been elected president.

Senator Daniel P. Moynihan should have been elected president.

The poor of America are wretches without dignity. They constitute an underclass that it is best to neglect, for only through the rigors of necessity can they achieve dignity in the last decades of the twentieth century as the Jews did in the first decades of this century.

True liberalism is that good old-time liberalism of the eighteenth century. Therefore it is the neoconservatives who are the true liberals of our time.

Judaism is now, and always has been, a conservative religion.

The demands for social justice of the Hebrew prophets played no part in the historic association of Jews with the left.

Overriding the ethical question for Jews is survival, which can only be guaranteed through the unabashed pursuit of Jewish interests; in other words, to get what you want, do whatever you have to do.

These tenets have been presented in a different light in *Commentary, The Wall Street Journal, The Public Interest,* and other outlets for neoconservative writing, many of which are subsidized by wealthy individuals and corporations, as well as in dozens of books. To say them stripped of argument and in shockingly ordinary language is brutal, I admit, but this brutality of presentation serves a purpose. By saying the tenets concisely it is possible to aggregate them, enabling the reader to consider the connections between the tenets and the character of the movement that holds them to be right and true.

Obviously, all neoconservatives would disagree with the manner in which their views have been presented. Some would argue that they do not subscribe to specific tenets; all would say that by stripping away the arguments, the ideas are made to appear harsh, cruel, unthinking.

A rationalizing context can be prepared for every argument, as any rhetorician knows. Furthermore, any movement may hold beliefs that are acceptable to most people when those beliefs are distinct and stated separately from the other beliefs of the movement; the classic example is the Nazi opposition to communism.

It is not the purpose of this book to present the views of the neoconservatives in the best light; that is the work of the publicists of the movement, and they have done it widely and well. My purpose here is to confront the movement with an older authority and to ask the reader, especially the Jewish reader, to decide whether the same person may comfortably hold both sets of beliefs.

The genesis of Jewish neoconservatism in his own life has been described by Norman Podhoretz in *Making It*, "My Negro Problem and Yours," *Breaking Ranks*, and other works that many Jews found embarrassing and without the universal application Mr. Podhoretz had imagined. In these works he speaks often, perhaps with unintended accuracy, of his "conversion," for he spent most of his early years of political awareness following the traditional Jewish ideas of mercy and social justice.

Publication of the confessions in *Making It* was a brave, ingenuous, and naive act. Had the book been written as fiction, Norman Podhoretz might now hold a place in American letters similar to that of Philip Roth. Instead, Norman Podhoretz became the intellectual version of Sammy Glick. The reviews of *Making It* were cruel, unforgiving of a still young man who had, like so many young critics, made no real connection with either art or life. Criticism of the critic was undoubtedly painful. The young editor and critic fought back, but he placed too much value on criticism; he fought too hard. His response was unbecoming, as the book had been unbecoming. The power of Norman Podhoretz was evanescent, the vulgarity remained.

Gossip about the neoconservative movement often attributes the conversion of Norman Podhoretz to the failure of his book, but that theory seems glib: This was not Herman Melville distraught over the reception of *Moby Dick*, nor was Norman Podhoretz merely a spiteful child turning on his old friends as he imagined they had turned on him, nor had an exceptionally bright and well-educated young man suddenly become a thick-witted street fighter. The book itself was the cause. The veneer of the Jewish intellectual was burned away in the writing; the vulgar man emerged and took up the appropriate philosophy.

With the distance of almost a dozen years, one can see the error in the construction of Mr. Podhoretz's position as clearly as a wrong move in a chess player's mid-game. The editor of "the Jewish intellectual monthly" thought Jews, and therefore Jewish ethics and culture, were vulgar. He confused the harsh surroundings of lower-middle-class and working-class life with the poverty of spirit of true vulgarity. Although he had been schooled in Jewish ethics and theology, the elegance of it was lost to him: How could true elegance speak broken English, live among black-skinned people, wear babushkas, eat chicken fat, and work in factories? Could an elegant person live in the back of the store? Could any outsider be anything but vulgar? If outsiders were not vulgar, why were they outsiders? To a man who had studied in England, his Russian forebears must have seemed strange indeed!

So Norman Podhoretz became something else, a new Saul of Tarsus breaking the yoke of the Law. But this new Saul did not replace the Law with the spirit; he chose the appetites. The elegance of the Jewish love of mercy had been replaced by the desire for power; the beauty of man's belief in social justice had been replaced by the vulgarity of self-interest. Mr. Podhoretz had written himself into a corner; in the years that followed he would devote his life to justifying and publicizing vulgarity, but not until he had converted the Jews would he be comfortable.

It was not difficult for Mr. Podhoretz to find allies and converts and to begin raising young Jews in the philosophy of neoconservatism. Events had become his conspirators:

Fear sat on the left hand of the neoconservatives, comfort sat on their right.

Many of the converts have told of the journey across the political spectrum, although not with the detail or the honesty of Norman Podhoretz. Most of the others have begun with rationalization rather than confession, attempting to hide their newfound preference for vulgarity. Almost all of them have said that it is because they are Jewish that they have become neoconservatives. They speak for each other; they help each other with grants, consulting fees, and introductions to money and power. It is a close camaraderie for all but Daniel Bell, who resigned as coeditor of *The Public Interest* after he and Irving Kristol founded the magazine, and who was given into the hands of Michael Novak in the July 1981 issue of *Commentary* to be drummed out of the corps as one whose "imagination still operates within a Marxian horizon." Novak, a Polish Catholic and the publicist of "ethnic interests," the new euphemism for racism, delivered the coup de grace earlier in the same paragraph: "Bell is said to have quipped that he is a liberal in politics, a socialist in economics, and a conservative in culture. The single most systematic strength in his thinking—and simultaneously, the single most glaring weakness—is that the socialist in him frequently overwhelms both the liberal and the conservative." The club is warm and supportive, but it is restricted. Daniel Bell, the best mind among the neoconservatives, cannot be considered a neoconservative: He simply could not bring himself to trade ethics for vulgarity.

For those Jews who made the complete journey, neoconservatism began with a misapplication of Hannah Arendt's work on totalitarianism, a misapplication in which she concurred. Arendt theorized that two of the most important steps on the way to a totalitarian state were the atomization and the massification of society. And so it was under Hitler and Stalin. The problem in Arendt's work is that she arrived

at theory by abstracting description, a problem she herself
recognized when she doubted that she had truly found the
origins of totalitarianism. She then applied the abstracted
description to America during the turmoil of the sixties, er-
roneously conflating America, Europe, and the Soviet
Union. In her misreading of America, the student radicals,
who could hardly agree on the day of the week or the time
of day, became massified man, the mob. In their jejune radi-
calism she saw the end of all cultural authority and morality. That much of their protest was against what they saw
as the more insidious forces of totalitarianism in American
society did not occur to her, and for good reason—she did
not know enough about life in America to understand what
the disorganized, incoherent children were pointing to.

Her misreading of the situation provided the jumping-off
point for the Jewish neoconservatives: The mob was coming
and it was coming out of the universities that had given the
Jews a way up out of the ghetto. Not just the road to respectability was under attack, however; the student radicals
were opposed to respectability itself. They did not want to
be Nathan Glazer or Sidney Hook or Daniel Bell or Irving
Kristol or Seymour Martin Lipset or Midge Decter or even
the editor of a Jewish intellectual monthly; ergo, they must
be communists.

It seems comic to describe this argument for the genesis
of neoconservatism, namely, the reaction of civilized men to
the student radicals, as merely petulant, but under the
theorizing, the quoting of statistics, and the defense of
Western civilization one finds mere petulance: The children
spat upon the accomplishments of the parents; only communism could lead them to such ingratitude, such madness.

Almost every one of the founders of Jewish neoconservatism produced a book or a major article about the student
radicals. Irving Kristol wrote an article for *Fortune* about
the prevalence of Jews among the student radicals. Mario

Savio and Tom Hayden did not figure prominently in his article: The attack on Jews by a Jew was to prove to the readers of *Fortune* that Jews were okay; they weren't all bearded radicals.

Social instability was bad for the Jews, said the Jewish neoconservatives; every time a nation went through a period of instability Jews suffered. They pointed to Hitler. They failed to point to Napoleon. They were frightened by the attacks on such historically benign institutions as universities. The breakdown of order in the streets and on the campuses reminded them of what they had read about Germany as the Nazis came to power. A repetition of history seemed possible. They sought to uphold the cultural authority that would prevent disaster for America—and particularly for American Jews. The radical students claimed to be following in the footsteps of the Hebrew prophets; the Jewish neoconservatives sought their authority in eighteenth-century liberalism.

Amid the turmoil of student riots on college campuses and in the streets of Chicago, the black radicals were having some trouble making themselves heard. The Black Panther organization, for example, was composed of four publicists, a handful of ex-convicts, and a great many motherly women, high school students, and junior high school students, a surprisingly large number of whom were physically handicapped. A major activity, perhaps the major activity, at the headquarters of the Black Panthers was the doling out of food money to shy, hungry, and deeply embarrassed middle-aged men. The money was given out by women, and the amounts were small and not accompanied by either moralizing or political propaganda. The Black Panthers, the most radical and vocal of the black groups claiming to be on the left, were heartbreaking, for they were a perfect reflection of the powerlessness of the black poor.

When the Black Panthers and a few other black radicals

announced their support for the Palestine Liberation Organization and their opposition to "Zionist imperialist racism," many Jews felt betrayed. They pointed to the long and deep Jewish involvement in civil rights, the two Jewish boys who had been murdered while trying to help bring civil rights to blacks in the South, and the Jewish financial support of civil rights organizations. And what did they get in return? Attacks on Israel, black anti-Semitism, the Jew-baiting poetry of LeRoi Jones. Jewish contributions to civil rights organizations stopped. The Jews who were to become the neoconservatives re-examined their relationship to blacks. They had always agreed with Cervantes' description of the world as composed of two families, the Haves and the Have-Nots, but they realized that Jews in America had moved into a new family and blacks had not.* The interests of the Haves are very different from those of the Have-Nots. Another step on the political journey to the right was taken.

* Many Jews have moved into the economic world of the Haves, but few, if any, have learned to feel the sense of security that is normally associated with the rich. All Jews are aware of anti-Semitism and all Jews are sensitive to it. One cannot, of course, look into another person's mind, but it seems likely that even those Jews who wholeheartedly embrace the interests of the Haves must do so by suppressing their knowledge of the true comfort of the rich, which is to know that they and their children are comfortable, powerful, and safe—and will remain so.

Jews may join the family of the Haves in the countinghouse, but the more profound distinction puts Jews among the Have-Nots. The quality of self-delusion required of a Jew who wishes to consider himself among the Haves has sometimes led to self-destructive behavior. Hannah Arendt has considered this problem along a parallel line in her discussion of the parvenu and the pariah. The behavior of Ronald Reagan toward Israel, Jewish lobbyists, Jacobo Timerman, and so forth, during the first year of his administration is an indication that Jewish support of his candidacy as the representative of the interests of the Haves may have been the kind of self-destructive behavior that comes of the failure to consider the profound conditions of one's life as the true conditions.

The new attitude toward blacks led to a new attitude toward affirmative action programs and public welfare. The Bakke case merely proved what Jewish neoconservatives had been saying for some time: A Have of greater merit could be displaced by a Have-Not of lesser merit. A disproportionate number of Jews went to the best colleges, universities, and professional schools. They went because the old quota system had been broken: Students were accepted on merit. A return to quotas would have the effect of displacing many Jews. Bizarre versions of bell-curve distributions were drawn and a great deal was written about the justice of merit systems; Herbert Spencer's formula of the survival of the fittest resonated in the prose.

A different view of government and the distribution of wealth came along with black support of the PLO and the fear of quota systems. Once the Jewish neoconservatives had found a good reason for ending their long association with the blacks, they could see the way to opposing the role of the federal government in many aspects of life. Business was for the Haves; government redistribution programs were not. If government had the power to regulate the workplace, the safety of products, and the use of the land, it was not a large step to ever stronger affirmative action programs—quotas.

The liberalism of the eighteenth century favored economic inequality—Leibniz had shown that inequality among men was the best of all possible worlds, for it reflected the inequality of creatures in nature—while the liberalism of the last third of the twentieth century was moving from equality of opportunity to equality of condition. Only a large and very powerful government could enforce equality of condition. Only a large and very powerful central government could redistribute wealth on an equal basis, and the Jews stood to lose a great deal in an equalizing of wealth.

In the language of the neoconservatives, all of this had to

do with Jewish interests. When they were still on the left, Jewish interests meant social justice, human rights, peace, a world in which mercy prevailed; but as they moved to the right, the definition of Jewish interests changed, becoming more parochial, more direct. The grand scheme would take care of itself; Jews had only to pursue their own self-interest to survive and prosper. Some neoconservatives went further, threatening that if Jews did not vigorously pursue their self-interests they might not prosper or even survive.

Among the chief Jewish interests, said the neoconservatives, was Israel, the tiny modern Western state in the Middle East, the Jewish homeland, the promised land. A Jew can interpret the meaning of Israel in many ways: The state is beleaguered, surrounded by large and ever more powerful enemies; Israel is David, invincible in battle; Israel is a great socialist experiment; the kibbutz was a small part of the settlement of the state, which is an ally of the noncommunist, capitalist West; Israel is the true home of all Jews of the world; Israel is a foreign country in which the majority of the population is Jewish; God gave Israel to the Jews; guns gave Israel to the Jews; Israel wants peace; Israel has become the modern Sparta; and so on and on. It is said that there are seventy interpretations of every word in the Bible; there are at least as many interpretations of the meaning of Israel.

All Jews want Israel to survive. There is no disagreement about the end. The disagreements between neoconservatives and other Jews center on the means and on the compromises in ethics American Jews must make to aid Israel under the Begin government. The neoconservatives came to two firm conclusions: First, there are no limits in regard to Israel;* the government of the state can do no wrong, nor

---

* See Ruth R. Wisse's interpretation of Y. L. Peretz's story about Yankele and the rabbi of Chelm of pp. 98–99 for an example of this kind of thinking.

can supporters of Israel err in moral choices if those choices
are made with the interests of Israel in mind; and second, a
politically conservative government in America would be
more likely to support Israel than a government that leaned
to the left. When John Connally, the favorite candidate of
big business in the 1980 presidential primaries, indicated his
willingness to trade Israel for Arab oil, the neoconservatives
did not pause to review their conclusion; they simply
switched their allegiance to Ronald Reagan, who was solid
on Israel.

The two conclusions on Israel as a Jewish interest fit
nicely with the other political positions that were becoming
more comfortable for these "converted" Jews; they could
openly ally themselves with the right wing of the Republican party. Before the 1980 presidential election *Commentary* devoted an issue to a symposium on "Liberalism & The
Jews." The symposium was heavily weighted toward the
right but included brief essays from Jewish social democrats. There was, of course, no consensus, but the majority
view was clear: Jewish interests had been redefined and
they were clearly on the right. Every argument in the symposium was tough-minded, almost chillingly secular, except
that of Michael Walzer, who still considered himself part of
a nation that began in an exodus from slavery in Egypt.

Now firmly aligned with those in power in America, the
Jewish neoconservatives have concluded their political
journey and may assume the role adumbrated in the writings
of Norman Podhoretz and Irving Kristol; they may become
the new court Jews, indispensable advisors who use their
influence with kings to protect the interests of other Jews.
In the past, court Jews had been financial advisors. Milton
Friedman might have fit that role, but not the new Jews.
They come from the social sciences (excepting Mr. Podhoretz), and while they consider themselves intellectuals,
with the broad range of knowledge of that modern descrip-

tion of the Renaissance man, they will have to bow to others for expert advice on economic policy, arms, the hard sciences, etcetera; their expertise will come in manipulating the public through policy and publicity. And they will be invaluable advisors, for they know that despite their protestations to the contrary, the increasingly unequal distribution of wealth under an administration with eighteenth-century economic, political, and social views must generate unrest among all but the favored few, leading to an increasing need for manipulation of the public to maintain power.

As court Jews they believe they can now deal most effectively with two of the issues that drove many of them to the right: the power of the Soviet Union and its anti-Semitic policies. The Jewish neoconservatives believe sincerely in the theory of Soviet plans for world dominance, and they believe with equal sincerity in the ability of the Soviet Union to achieve and hold the lead in both nuclear and conventional capabilities to wage war. As they observed the Soviet arms buildup of the last twenty years and heard the social democrats, New Leftists, and the liberal wing of the Democratic party discuss overkill, nuclear parity, cutbacks in military spending, and other ideas that seemed to them closer to pacifism or surrender than to defense, they became frightened. The ruling group in the Soviet Union made no secret of its anti-Semitism, refusing to permit Jews to emigrate at will, limiting Jewish attendance at institutions of higher education, barring the printing of Jewish prayer books, and forcing Jews to carry identity cards stating that they were Jews.

Life for Jews in a world conquered by the Soviet Union is the nightmare of the Jewish neoconservatives. They believe —and not entirely without reason—that world conquest by the Soviet Union would lead to the destruction of the Jews. The nightmare drives them; they are willing to do almost anything to keep it from becoming reality; it overshadows their thinking on all issues.

Many of the firstlings of Jewish neoconservatism came from the anticommunist left. Some of them—like Irving Kristol in his article in *Commentary* in 1952—were sympathetic to the McCarthy investigations even when they were leftists. They believed in the cold war and distrusted détente. They were certain that the United States would be bested by the Russians in the negotiation of an arms limitation treaty. Anticommunism was their birthright; they did not have to be converted to it. The conversion of anticommunist leftists to anticommunist conservatives came in the search for allies and in the fear that a politically and culturally volatile nation was vulnerable to revolution or defeat.

Finally, they came to believe that the best defense against communism was not socialism but capitalism, for capitalism was not only the economic antithesis of communism, it was the religious antithesis. The connection between capitalism and religion had been made by Tawney and Weber, as well as by Hooker, Calvin, and Smith: The survival of the Jews depended upon the survival of religion.

There are a great many leaps in the reasoning of the Jewish neoconservatives, but they cannot be criticized for lacking a systematic approach. Neoconservatism is a popular movement, not a political philosophy. As such, it is made up of pieces of political and economic systems tied together with a little hope and a lot of fear. Movements, unlike philosophies, thrive on emotion. They need publicists rather than popularizers, for they begin as popularizations of sophisticated ideas. No one can debate a movement, because it has no rules. Peter Steinfels argued brilliantly against the tenets of the movement in his book *The Neo-Conservatives,* but to dispute the discrete tenets of a movement is like cutting one leaf from each branch of an oak tree; the trunk and the roots will not notice the wound.

As a movement Jewish neoconservatism has roots somewhat different from those told in the articles, essays, and confessions of its adherents. Most of the reasons given so far for the rightward movement of Jews can be found in back issues of *Commentary* or in the works of various Jewish neoconservative spokesmen. Some other reasons—not necessarily damaging to the movement or its founders and adherents—should also be considered, for movements are not made by rational decisions, conversions do not necessarily take place in the soul, and personal choices are not made in the absence of history and circumstance. We respond to our lives; we are something when we make those responses.

Norman Podhoretz, when he was the movement's memoirist, said in *Breaking Ranks* that those who did not pursue their interests acted out of self-hatred. More recently, speaking as the movement's military affairs expert in *The Present Danger*, he said that neoconservatives might more accurately be described as neonationalists, partly because of their "highly positive" view of American values. The essential difference, according to Mr. Podhoretz, between those who remained left liberals and those who became neoconservatives is that left liberals hate themselves and their country while neoconservatives love themselves and their country. In other words, the difference is between the optimists and the pessimists, between those who are very critical of themselves and their country—because they think both can be improved—and those who believe they live in the best of all possible countries.

How did the Jewish neoconservatives come to believe in contemporary America as the best of all possible nations? Surely they did not read Leibniz and decide to find the best of all possible worlds in one country. They must have observed something in America, and in their own circumstances, that so profoundly pleased them as to cause their conversion.

What they saw was America, the only country of its kind on earth, hardly a melting pot, more like a stewpot in which the various ingredients remain discrete while imparting something of their flavor to each other. No single ingredient dominated the stew as in virtually all other nations. The country they saw was predominantly white and Christian, but the whites were ethnically diverse and the Christians were of every known variety. Without a modicum of ethnic and religious tolerance to give it the semblance of a cohesive nation, the state could not function. With relatively little reluctance Jews were included in the general tolerance. It created an opportunity to prosper as never before, and they prospered. The men who were to become neoconservatives had an epiphany; they could, as Mr. Podhoretz said, make it.

Jews had made it before in other countries: Rothschilds, Sassoons, some German Jews, some Spanish Jews before the Inquisition. But this time it seemed that they could do more than make it; they could keep it. Even more astonishing was the requirement for making it in America: a little work, a little luck, nothing more. Ordinary men, even if they were Jews, could live extraordinarily well in America. They could be rich.

When a man who was born poor gets rich, it seems like a miracle to him. When a man who was born rich discovers that other men were born poor, his own riches seem like a blessing to him. There is a natural connection between God and good fortune that leads the rich to think God is on their side. They do not ask questions prepared for them by Job or Qoheleth. The rich also have a different conception of God, as exemplified in the works of Calvin, Spencer, and Adam Smith: They view Him as just but not merciful, for they do not need His mercy.

A man who spends his life looking down at other men feels different from a man who goes through his days looking up: He feels more than a little closer to heaven than other men. Since he believes justice has been done by making him comfortable, he develops a moral view that enables him, in good conscience, to conserve his position. It all seems quite natural to him, for God made lions and the prey of lions and the creatures who beautify the preserve of lions by eating the aftermath of the lions' feasts. That is the order of life. For the lion a change in the order means either having less to eat or living with the possibility of being eaten. He lives with luxury and pessimism. And if he is the Lion of Judah, he also enjoys his power under the shadow of history.

The Jewish neoconservatives did not come capriciously to their epiphany; they studied the evidence as their university professors had trained them to do. By the time of their conversions, the need for massive charity to aid poor Jews in America had come to an end. Jewish charity now went to Israel. The Lower East Side of New York and Maxwell Street in Chicago still had a slightly Jewish flavor, but the tenements above the remaining Jewish shops were now occupied by blacks, Mexicans, and Puerto Ricans. The ghetto was gone. Henry Roth had been replaced by Philip Roth. Jews no longer lived in coal cellars or walked down the hall to the communal toilet or the communal water faucet. The women in the sweatshops now spoke Spanish or Chinese.

Not all Jews were rich, but on New York's Upper West Side the old men and old women sitting on benches on Broadway were easy to overlook because they were old. Those who lived behind locked and bolted doors, afraid to live and afraid to die, aging in maddening loneliness, asked, by their hiding, to be overlooked for fear of who might find them. The middle-aged, middle-class Jewish founders of neoconservatism do not live in the world, nor do they seem to believe it when they see it, preferring instead the world that comes to them cooked and ready to eat in the form of statistics.

The statistics gave the evidence needed to look down on the world of the poor. Jews were among the most affluent people in America; only Irish Catholics came close to them as an ethnic group. No group sent a higher percentage of its young to universities. Jews had achieved majority status on the faculty of Harvard University. Jews were not the only people who noted the new statistics, nor were they the only ones who exaggerated their meaning. By ignoring the fact that most of the statistics reflected the per capita status of a very small number of people or the uniqueness of the situation at Harvard, Jews could be made to appear to wield great power. Paul N. McCloskey, Jr., a Republican congressman from California, went so far as to tell a group of retired military officers in July, 1981, "We've got to overcome the tendency of the Jewish community in America to control the actions of Congress and force the President and the Congress not to be evenhanded . . ."

Representative McCloskey was not the first conservative in government to misuse the statistics. The chairman of the Joint Chiefs of Staff had said that Jews controlled the media in America. There had been other statements, less official, less publicized, but the statistics claimed that anti-Semitism, except among blacks, was fading in America. The personal experiences of the leaders of the Jewish move to the right confirmed the statistics on anti-Semitism. Richard Nixon spoke of Midge Decter as one of his favorite dinner guests. Intimates of Ronald Reagan speak of how well Mr. Reagan and "Nate" Glazer got on at their first meeting, a meeting at which Nancy Reagan joined Richard Nixon as a member of Midge Decter's fan club. Norman Podhoretz was described

as "cold" during that same meeting. "He was slow to come
around to Reagan, but now he's on the inside." The implica-
tion of opportunism on the part of Mr. Podhoretz notwith-
standing, it was not easy for Jews to come around to supporting Republican candidates, especially Ronald Reagan, a
man whose politics fluctuated between conservative and reactionary. It was a long way from Jacob Javits to Ronald
Reagan, farther than most Jews—born into a tradition of left
liberalism—could travel, or so it seemed. The Jewish vote in
the 1980 presidential election proved that Jews could join
the rest of America in following what appeared to be their
interests. Jimmy Carter, friend of Israel, the man who had
labored over the Camp David accords, was the first Democratic candidate since 1924 not to receive a majority of the
Jewish vote. Ronald Reagan did not receive a majority either. One of every seven Jews voted for John Anderson,
leaving Mr. Reagan with only 39 percent of the Jewish vote,
but it was still a great victory for Jewish interests—and not
for love of Israel or concern for the human rights of Jews in
the Soviet Union or Argentina; Jimmy Carter had proved
himself on both issues and Ronald Reagan was not only
untried but belonged to the party of John Connally, who
was willing to trade Jews for oil, and Jerry Falwell, who
didn't think Jews could get into heaven because God didn't
hear their prayers. The interests that prevailed among Jews
were the interests of the family of the Haves.

The behavior of the Reagan administration toward Israel
raises doubts about the judgment of the Jewish leaders of
the neoconservative movement; and even though it seems
cruel to say, the Reagan policies are so in keeping with the
political and economic thinking of the right that one must
ask whether the neoconservatives were clear about their
motives when they gave their support to Reagan and the
right. What proof did they have that Reagan had any incli-
nation to follow the special view of Israel as a moral issue

that has characterized American foreign policy for more than thirty years? They knew his view of human rights: He was not even neutral; he was more than willing to trade a few lives to keep an anticommunist regime in power, and neither he nor his ambassador to the United Nations ever specified that they be non-Jewish lives.

What really came first for the Jewish neoconservatives? If it was not their own economic interest, if it was Israel, they must have been such naïfs at politics or so blinded by their sudden connection to the Haves as to construct the plot of their own betrayal. By the ninth month of the Reagan administration the New York *Times* reported that both Norman Podhoretz and Irving Kristol were complaining of their lack of influence in decisions on policy. By the tenth month the Administration was using the assassination of Anwar Sadat as a reason for selling AWACS to the Saudis, and Secretary Haig, perhaps for effect, was describing Egypt as America's foremost ally in the Middle East.

Another aspect of the journey to the right that does not appear in the published writings of the Jewish guides on the trip is the momentum of the change itself. As Nathan Glazer had once said, "Jews are a people of the left." When they abandoned that position, with its ethical, historical, and cultural authority, they were set adrift. In the beginning of their journey they must have suffered a kind of cultural weightlessness more terrible than loneliness. They whirled around each other, the entire movement buffeted by events. They opposed the counterculture, they opposed the New Left; what could they say about the war in Vietnam? They opposed the blacks; what could they say to the racist theories of looney scientists and trash preachers? The twentieth century displeased them; the nineteenth century displeased them; they found a foothold in the eighteenth century and looked longingly at the political and social ideas of ancient Greece. Old friends shunned

them; they looked for new friends. Jews from Brooklyn,
who prepped among poor blacks in public high schools, and
Jews with Lower East Side intonations in their voices,
whose undergraduate clubs had been corner tables in cafe-
terias, told themselves that they were welcome in America's
WASP establishment. Without ethics, culture, or history to
whisper the antidote to flattery, they did not know who
they were. They moved on, each move determining the
next. By 1981 they orchestrated a merciless attack on the
character of a Jew who had been tortured with electric
shocks and anti-Semitic execration—Jacobo Timerman.

Nathan Glazer claims a growing response to the Holocaust as one of the reasons Jews moved to the right. The
formulation has the soundness of a burn victim claiming he
can only pour gasoline safely while smoking a cigarette. Yet
Mr. Glazer is undoubtedly correct. A rational response to
the Holocaust is, as Tadeusz Borowski showed in his stories
of life in a death camp, the greatest madness. The upheaval
in a Jew's soul that comes with the thought of the Holocaust
gives rise to fearful blind crashings that defy interpretation.
After the Holocaust all Jews must ask, Why should we be
merciful? Who was merciful to us? If those questions lead a
Jew to abandon mercy, is he still a Jew?

If a man confuses power and morality, riches and righteousness, cruelty and justice, the charity of Herbert Spencer
and the charity of Deuteronomy, is he a Jew? Is a person
without mercy a Jew because his parents were Jews or because he chooses to call himself a Jew?

Jews of the left and the right have argued that the politics of a man in the twentieth century must not be determined by ancient prophets. Then what of ethics? And if not
ethics, then what is religion? If Moses had seen a Jew beating an Egyptian workman, what would he have done? According to Rashi's count, the answer is found thirty-six times

in the Pentateuch; that is how much importance Scripture lays on the prohibition against the mistreatment of a stranger. And if the Egyptian were a slave rather than just a stranger, the answer would be the same and the statements of the prohibition would also be numerous.*

Judaism has always been the same, and no two Jews have ever agreed on what it is. The Law has been spoken and written, defined and redefined, interpreted and reinterpreted so many times that no man living can fully know every definition and interpretation. It has been touched by every major philosophical system, from the idealism of Plato to the mystical existentialism of Martin Buber, and the colorations of it have only just begun. Archaeologists have traced YHWH to a Midianite volcano god. Freud theorized the murder of Moses the father by his child horde. Genesis is thought to be an old tale told by desert tribes. There is no history of Judaism that agrees with any other history. We have endured countless messiahs and we are still waiting for the Messiah. We gave birth to Christianity and Islam and lived to see both religions try to extinguish the flame that begot them.

Discussion of the irreconcilable problems of interpretation of the Law was carried to such extremes that the word *pilpul* came to mean fruitless hairsplitting. And still we argued, as if one could find not only the truth but the truth of the truth, as if the discussion could be completed and the religion could be laid to rest, as if the true religion of the Jews did not exist in the discussion itself.

Somewhere there are constants, an essence, a light like the light above the Ark that cannot be extinguished. Every Jew is empowered to describe the light. The attempt at description is not hubris but study. Any Jew may dispute the

---

* Another source for the answer is the story of Moses and the sheep, told in the talmudic commentary on Exodus: It is because Moses shows compassion that God chooses him to lead His flock.

description, but it is a tenet of the religion of equals that no man can say with absolute certainty that any other man's description is wrong.

Now a new political movement has come to Judaism, a movement of self-interest, without mercy for the old or the poor, a movement that condemns oppression only when it serves the interests of the movement to do so. Perhaps that is the fitting description of the light in our time. It must be compared with the Judaism that has endured to find out whether it is the seventy-first interpretation of the words of the Law or the beginning of a new religion.

2. The Christmas Tree Massacre

It does not snow in San Francisco. The Christmas season looks like any other. Only the windows of the department stores change to herald the buying of mandatory gifts. It is also possible that in a town of many drunks there are more drunks, or more people are drunk more often, during the Christmas season. Those are the signs of the celebration of the birth of Jesus as an adult might notice them in San Francisco.

Children, we are told, or think we remember, have a different view. Visions of sugarplums are said to dance in their heads. My sons had never seen a sugarplum, to my knowledge. Neither had I. Nevertheless, being a Jew in a land where most people celebrated the birth of Jesus and the mythical beneficence of Santa Claus, I inspected my children's eyes, expecting the visions of sugarplums to be manifest in a twinkle. The inspections revealed two pairs of eyes, standard issue, one pair green, one pair brown.

It was sufficient for me. I had never celebrated Christmas and I never planned to. Nor had I or anyone in my family made a great fuss about Ḥanukah, a minor Jewish festival that usually falls in December. The history behind the festival was interesting, the melody of the blessing was an easy one to recall, but it was a pale festival. I didn't build a sukkah on the roof of the apartment house and run around waving palm fronds, willow, myrtle, and citron for a week; I saw no reason to become excited over the celebration of Ḥanukah. The case was closed for Christmas and for transmogrifications of Christmas.

We must have seen something that looked like a twinkle in one of the children's eyes, probably in one of the green eyes, since the brown eyes were only two years old. Perhaps the twinkle appeared in the green eyes during the celebration on December 8 of the brown-eyed son's birthday. We bought a Christmas tree. It was the smallest Christmas tree in San Francisco in deference to the fact that it was not purchased by Christians. According to the man who sold us the tree, it was two feet tall. San Francisco is a city of hyperbole. I told my wife the tree was two feet tall. She said it looked very short.

Placed upon a table in a corner of the living room, the tree did not seem short at all; it dominated the room, touching the walls, casting shadows up to the ceiling. The odor of the tree permeated the rooms of the apartment. We seemed to be living in a pine forest, a Gentile pine forest.

Despite its enormity, the tree did not have the flavor of Christmas about it. We were dissatisfied. I argued that a Christmas tree would never be a Christmas tree in a Jewish home. My wife suggested that it needed decorations, things to hang from the branches, a star for the top.

If it's a six-pointed star, I said.

We agreed not to have a star.

I'll put a latke on the top and hang dreidels from the branches.

We went to the dime store to buy proper decorations for the enormous tree: lights, shiny balls, tinsel, whatever the dime store had for sale. All the decorations appeared to be religious symbols, from the angels holding missals to the completeplasticcrèchereusableyearafteryear to the markings on the box of tinsel. We bought Christian tinsel, uncircumcised lights, and shiny cruciform balls.

None of us knew exactly what to do with the decorations. Once, in Texas, I had helped an elderly neighbor to decorate a Christmas tree, but it had been a long time ago. All I remembered was changing the light bulbs over and over until all the strings of lights were lit. I could not remember the order of hanging the decorations. We decided to hang the cruciform balls, then the uncircumcised lights, and finally the tinsel. The red, blue, gold, and silver balls were surprisingly light and delicate. They did not weigh heavily on the branches.

While winding the string of lights through the branches, I knocked one of the balls down, cutting my hand. Although the cut did not appear to be very deep and the color of the blood showed that I had not cut an artery, it was very difficult to stop the bleeding. My blood is ordinarily as thick as heavy cream and clots as easily, but on that night it ran out of my veins.

God had not come on a mission to my house before. I do not expect divine interventions in my life, but when I awakened in the middle of the night with a sore throat, clogged nose, and what felt like a bit of fever, I wondered whether God had taken notice of me at last.

Early the next evening, my green-eyed son, while wandering among the great branches of the Christmas tree, broke another of the cruciform balls. His hand was cut so deeply that stitches were required to close the wound. On the way home from having him sewed up, I resolved to save the lives of the Shorris family by getting the Christmas tree out of my house. Like David approaching the giant of Gath in the valley of Elah, I advanced upon the Goliath of Christmas trees. For a moment I was afraid, but I knew that righteousness was on my side and I snatched the great tree from its moorings and bore it out to the trash bin. Disregarding the mystical signs that hung from its limbs, I broke it in half with my bare hands and cast it down into the dark barrel, the Sheol of Christmas trees. Then all the family—the mother, the wounded men, and even the babe—rejoiced.

Jean-Paul Sartre's *Anti-Semite and Jew* brought a surprising message to me. I found out that I did not exist. Worse yet, I found out that if I had existed I would have had no history. And if I had appeared on earth through some sort of spontaneous generation, only to suffer an inauthentic existence, my life would have been about as rich and interesting as that of a mollusk; for, according to Sartre, being a Jew I would have had no culture. A Jew could only be a Jew, in Sartre's view, if he could say with Jeremiah, "I am the man who has been through trouble," and if the trouble was not caused by his own luck or stupidity or by acts of other Jews.

Sartre said Jews were sort of nice people, but this kindness fit in with the rest of his theory. If a group of people are defined as victims, one would expect a gentleness in their character. Who's afraid of a victim? If a victim was anything but sweet and passive, he wouldn't be a victim.

It is unfair to Sartre not to say that he also prescribed for the lack of authentic existence, history, and culture of Jews. He was a staunch anti-anti-Semite, which means I could have counted him a friend if I had existed. On the other hand, if there were no anti-Semites I would not even exist inauthentically; how would he know how to find me to be my friend?

The most disturbing part about Sartre's little book is that it is, in large measure, correct. Jews have a history, and a rich one, whether Sartre and Hegel think so or not. We are also possessed of a culture so broad and so deep that it can be divided into Hebrew and Yiddish Jewish culture, or into parochial and universalistic culture, and so on. One must stretch the definition of a culture to include both an American Reform Jew and an Israeli Ḥasid. The conflation of Orthodox Jews from an East European shtetl with the Sephardim of England presents an equally difficult problem in the definition of culture. Perhaps what Sartre meant to say is that some highly assimilated Jews, including many who have intermarried and converted, or converted for other reasons, do not have a strong culture entirely their own, and even that seems difficult to believe. One can argue with Sartre about history and culture, but the definition of Jews by anti-Semitism carries more than a little truth.

One can say simply that a man is known by his enemies: Anti-Semites are much more concerned with Jews than those who have no prejudice. Anti-Semites gave Jews the ghetto, a place to develop a culture separate from the culture of the surrounding world, a convenience to culture if not to life. Jews had no choice but to be Jews or to die. If such an existence is inauthentic, all existence is inauthentic, for no man is given any greater choice in society: Either he obeys its rules or the society will not permit him any life except that of prisoner or exile.

The larger and more proper issue Sartre raises is about society itself. He brands anti-Semitism on the class system as a sign of its profound corruption, a "bourgeois representation of the class struggle." He goes on to identify the roots of anti-Semitism in the pursuit of interests: "It can exist only in a society where a rather loose solidarity unites strongly structured pluralities"; he says that "it is a phenomenon of social pluralism." Sartre argues for a well-intentioned universalism—exactly the opposite of the argument of Norman Podhoretz and Irving Kristol, the proponents of the pursuit of narrow interests in a pluralistic society.

Does Sartre wish to do away with the Jews through the creation of a homogeneous society? He does not give a clear answer to the question. Do the Jewish neoconservatives wish to foment anti-Semitism as the savior of Judaism? They would, of course, say they wish nothing more fervently than to bring an end to anti-Semitism. They would point to Madison's praise of a variety of interests balancing each other in the maintenance of the republic, conveniently forgetting that Madison warned against the danger of factions, a warning that can be found in Sartre's theory of the cause of anti-Semitism.

The question a Jew must ask of himself if he is to look in his inner mirror and find his existence authentic is whether he would be a Jew if he could be something else. Jews have often had such a choice. Saul of Tarsus offered the Jews the choice. The Spanish Inquisition offered the choice in a more forceful manner. Christianity has always been open to Jews. In the Soviet Union Jews may now choose to give up their identity as Jews, or so it is said officially. Jews disappear from Judaism in America whenever they like.

Is a Jew bound to Judaism by his nose? A plastic surgeon can make a nose to please the person who wears it.

Circumcision is almost universal in America.

Jews have the same range of skin tone as other Caucasians.

Jews speak English, most of them with regional accents. Only Ḥasidic Jews and very Orthodox Jews can be distinguished by their dress, and even for them it is not difficult to shave a beard or remove a yarmulke.

Sartre's theory does not apply to millions of American Jews. Or does it? Whether the idea of inauthentic existence leads to comedy or to a profound understanding of man is a question that can be put aside to give room to consideration of the more useful part of Sartre's argument. Why, for example, is God said to have chosen the Jews? There were other nations available to him. The Egyptians had considered monotheism. There is some evidence that the Midianites were close to the same idea. The high culture of Greece could have been directed to the answers of monotheism instead of the questions of philosophy. Instead of already great civilizations, he chose the Jews, a small people, utterly powerless, disorganized, living in slavery in a foreign land. Was it to tell man something about God's politics that He looked to the lowest level of society to find a people to carry His word? Or was it to say something about being chosen that He appeared to the Jews at their lowest ebb?

And why did He choose one people rather than ten or two or everyone on earth? If God is God, and there was a time when men thought He intervened in earthly affairs, surely every option conceivable to man (and some conceivable only to God) was open to Him. Yet He chose but one of the peoples of the world, and He could not have chosen a much more humble people than a group of slaves in exile— worse than in exile, without a country.

Let us assume that God's choice was not capricious, since caprice is a human characteristic and we would not want a god who was merely human. Then we can attempt to ascribe some meaning to the choice. The possibilities of a small people becoming powerful among nations were small, perhaps nil, sparing the Chosen People the corruption of holding power among nations, although not the corruption of power within the nation. A divine view of the power of nations was made clear, implying a warning.

In choosing slaves, God made a sweeping political state-

ment: He knew of the existence of the poor and He did not
shun them or neglect them. He chose instead to give them a
way to change the status quo, to escape from oppression, to
be free from the political and economic bonds of slavery.
One can infer from the choice of the Jews that their Libera-
tor was not satisfied with the political economy of Egypt
and therefore chose to disturb it, that it was not His will either to preserve the power of kings or to maintain a human
order like the natural order, giving the weak over to the
strong to be used for the benefit of the strong. Justice for
man was to be different from the justice of nature.

How were the Chosen People defined before they were
chosen? We do not really know. The Bible is unclear on the
question. We do know, however, that in the desert the
frightened Hebrews built a golden calf. We know, too, that
the Law does not assume monotheism. Perhaps the Jews felt
some lingering monotheism that could be traced back to
Abraham. Perhaps they had been influenced by the brief
period of monotheism in Egypt. Since they had not yet been
given the Law, we can be sure that the Hebrews who went
into the desert were not the same as those who entered the
promised land. In fact, the forty years of wandering was to
serve as a religious and cultural purgative.

The Chosen People had already been chosen by circumstance. They were defined from outside, for no man chooses
to be a slave—the condition is thrust upon him. The genesis
of the people whom God chose was from outside. They
were a nation made by their enemies. It could be argued
that in choosing the Hebrew slaves and giving them the
Law God was giving them the opportunity to have an authentic existence. But why, then, choose a small, weak people, one destined always to be one of the least among nations? No matter how rich or cohesive it became, no matter
how positively it identified itself from within, the nation of
the Hebrews would always have a passive definition as well.

Did God choose a people that would have to live in such circumstances merely to be certain that the people He chose would remain His? Was He so unsure of His choice? He had the option of choosing all the people of the earth, of making man His chosen among the species instead of making the Hebrews His chosen among men. The external definition Jews have lived with since they were slaves in Egypt must have more meaning than mere inauthenticity.

The existence described by Sartre and determined by the circumstance of being chosen may have more to do with ethics than existentialism. The Jews were destined from the moment they entered into the Covenant to be separate from other peoples, differing from all others by their acceptance of the Covenant. It must be remembered that the Covenant defined their relation to God, not to men. Jews were to act toward other men according to the Law. Nothing in the Covenant even suggested how other men would react to a chosen people.

How could non-Jews react to a people who claimed to have been set apart by God except to agree to the distinctiveness of Jews? And how could those who were not chosen react to a people who claimed to be chosen except with envy in its many forms? A pariah nation had been created in the desert, the macrocosm of the life the Jew would come to know as an individual in the Diaspora.

As Leo Baeck understood so well, the pariah always sits on the left side in parliament. He has no choice but to be the opposition; the powerful have made him so by making him a pariah. He must develop his ethics from that position. He must love mercy, for mercy is his life. He must seek the rule of law and the limits of power or he may forfeit his life. He must be the publicist of ethics among all men, if only to save himself. Such is the life of the pariah, the man defined by his enemies, the one who lives inauthentically.

Or does the Jew choose to be a pariah? Has he learned to

love the ethical life that was thrust upon him in the desert more than three thousand years ago? It has always been the Jew's choice to be a Jew and to teach his children to be Jews. If Sartre had not stripped the Jew of his history in considering his existence, he might have realized that the Jew chooses his life in the most profound way, for his history tells him that his choice may be his undoing. Then it would have been Sartre and not us who faced the question: Is the man who exists inauthentically by his own choice not truly living authentically?

What kind of man, knowing this about himself, can say he has always been pleased to be a Jew?

We make the choice so early in the world that it often seems like the history of someone else. We learn to be pleased to be one of many, but not too many. A man gains a sense of himself by being different. If the outsides of humans all looked as alike as livers or lungs, we could not be individuals; we would be more like ants or clams, which are more like each other. None of us admires the physical life of the ant or the clam, much less the social life. Why should we admire the intellectual life? To be different, but not so different as to be alone, gives men the perspective of viewing the world from separate angles. It is very much like having two eyes.

To be a Jew gives a man a hint of how to live as if he were made in the image of a perfect being. If there is no justice, he will be the first to suffer injustice. If there is no mercy, he will be the first to suffer cruelty. Only if justice is presumed to be the opposite of mercy will he enjoy the fruits of justice. The temptation to be unjust, cruel, or to make justice the opposite of mercy is less for a Jew than for most men—at first, for selfish reasons. However, a man can move beyond selfishness, he can learn to define himself by his ethics; if only he can begin, if only he has the luck to have lessons soon enough in his life.

It has not often been admitted, but some Jews are pleased by the very difficulty of being a Jew. They find the relentless discomfort a spur, a heightening of the awareness of being alive. Mountain climbers and racing-car drivers claim a similar pleasure in putting themselves at risk. All daredevils know the thrall of danger. A Jew can find it at a cocktail party or a business lunch when an anti-Semitic remark suddenly comes into the conversation. His nerves sing with tension, a chill comes into his gut, he fears himself, the chance that he will fail this test of his courage, of his sense of himself. The moment does not endanger his physical life, but he feels the threat to his humanness, to his dignity; and he knows that without dignity he turns into a thing that can be bought and sold, he returns to the time before his exodus from Egypt.

Jews are a mystery to many Gentiles, although less so in America now. Perhaps no other people on earth has revealed so much of itself, told so many of its guilts and secret fears, yet there remain educated Gentiles who think Jews are a separate race. Others are certain that Jews own the banks or Wall Street or both. We are thought to have secret, strange rituals, perhaps having to do with the blood of Christian children, perhaps with some hooknosed manifestation of the devil. We are known as misers and spendthrifts, clean and dirty, bookish, gentle, social climbers, aggressive, loud, clannish, usurers, cowards, spartans. We are not all things to all people, but we are surely all things to some people.

A black friend asked me why it was that the best violinists were always Jewish. I said it was because we have rhythm. The friendship cooled. It was the first inkling for him that the color of Jews is white but the life circumstance is somewhere between black and white. He had always enjoyed playing the role of outsider and he did not like the idea of a man with white skin enjoying the same role.

To be a minority takes away, but it also gives. Having secrets or having people think he has secrets gives a man plumage. It may even invest him with an aura of the arcane knowledge of the outsider. Henry Kissinger plays his accent. I have known Jews who played dark circles under their eyes, Lower East Side origins, Yiddishisms, even hooked noses. In a crowded world sameness eliminates great quantities of people and things from consideration. One wishes for a distinguishing characteristic to protest his uniqueness. Even Hollywood now looks for irregular names and unfamiliar faces. To be a Jew provides a step toward consideration, although not always of the most pleasant kind.

Choosing to be a Jew may necessitate more than a mere declaration if one wishes to make a paradox of Sartre's theory by existing as more than another's object. A man may have declared himself a Jew at the age of thirteen, given some time to study of the Law, or even developed the habit of attending services in a synagogue and still not be a Jew because he denies the ethics of a small and humble people who claim to be God's chosen.

A man who declares himself a Jew and also declares that mercy is the opposite of justice negates the first declaration with the second. He denies both the history and the ethics that necessarily follow upon the history of the Jews. He makes himself both a Jew and not a Jew. He becomes the truly inauthentic man, defined from without and denying even that definition from within. Such a man has abandoned himself as well as his people. He floats on the surface of society, propelled by his own appetites. All that he has permitted himself he has also made permissible to those who are more powerful than Jews will ever be.

3. An Uncle in Spats, An Uncle in Shul

After many years the uncles of childhood come to have the uncertain reality of people met in books. They are not like characters in movies; the scale of them is human and they wear their own faces. The uncles of childhood live in the mixed distances of memory and imagination, like the creatures invented in books and given to the reader for completion. They differ only in that they smell of soup and taste of dill. Uncles and characters in books are stories who would like to be myths; they want to tell us how to live. The most favored question of uncles is, What do you want to be when you grow up?

Uncles, like characters in books, may be known as much by their meaning as by their being. Categories apply to them. They do not fit precisely, of course, since they are human, but if we apply something akin to structuralist abstraction to them, if we look beyond the obvious and the real, discarding all that does not properly abstract, we may put them neatly into categories and use them to examine ourselves. My economic uncles, Henry and Phillip, belong to the same category and tell the same story by different lives.

HENRY

Henry lived his home life among the feebleminded, the sickly, the obese, and the loutish. He looked at them all through the windows of a pince-nez.

How Henry came to live such a life is not clear. Overheard gossip and vague answers to a child's questions produce this series of events: As a young man in Persia Henry entered the diplomatic service. He was almost perfectly suited to the work: tall and slim, with the posture of a British officer; a dark, handsome young man, already beginning to develop deep vertical creases in his face. He wore celluloid collars and spats. His nose was constructed to be pinched by a pair of eyeglasses joined by a piece of spring steel. He handled the device with aplomb.

There is no way to know what young Henry, with his slightly British accent, expected of the Persian diplomatic corps. Adventure? Advancement? A life of elegance and aplomb? Perhaps he would have been comfortable somewhere in the British Empire. He was sent to Chicago to be the Persian consul in that city so different in character from my uncle Henry that he must have thought at times of the relative civilization of darkest Africa.

Not long after Henry was posted to Chicago, there was a revolution in Persia. Everything about the country of his birth changed, even its name. Henry could not return to Persia, which no longer existed, and Iran had no use for him in Chicago. He became an American. His problem as a new citizen of America was how to earn a living. He could no longer be a diplomat, so he did what any man trained in the art of diplomacy would do: He became a salesman of burial plots.

Henry did well with his aplomb. He married a beautiful young woman who, as the eldest of six children, had a certain stateliness befitting Henry's style. After delivering her second child, the stately young woman contracted encephalitis, which she is said to have passed on to her infant son through her milk. The bacillus nearly killed them. The fever destroyed much of the son's brain, leaving him a child for life. The mother was left with a severe tremor and a speech defect. She gave the impression of bovine rumination. A permanent squint grew in the faces of the hurt mother and her hurt son, as if they were pained in consideration of themselves.

The hope that Henry's daughter would marry well began when she was a small child, for she was more beautiful than her mother had been and she was blessed with the elegance and bearing of her father. The most eligible young men courted her. They appealed to her father, they begged for her hand. She spurned them all, preferring a man with a narrow mustache and slickly black hair, a horseplayer and sometime driver of taxicabs. During her first pregnancy she became obese. Afterward she continued to increase in size. It was said of her husband the horseplayer that he liked big women. It was said of her that one could still see in her face that she had been a beauty. Her first child developed the habit of sniffing his food like an animal before deciding whether to eat it. For a long time he would eat nothing but canned salmon.

The other member of Henry's household was his mother-in-law, a widow. She had yellow-and-white hair and the face of a dowager angel. She was from Königsberg, a Prussian, and it showed in her bearing and in her unassailable dignity. Like Henry she belonged to a different time and a different life. She had nothing. She had been penniless for years, the ward of her children in the house of her son-in-law. She dressed herself in the old culture. She was not effusive. Much of her life was spent alone in her darkened room at the far end of Henry's sprawling apartment.

There was seldom any peace in Henry's house. The horse-player teased his feebleminded brother-in-law. The child who sniffed his food played at the grand piano in the living room, picking out popular tunes by ear, momentarily deluding the family into thinking a musical genius had been born to the horseplayer and the obese woman. Another child had been born to the horseplayer and his wife, a girl, who also played at the piano. Often she and her brother played simultaneously while the horseplayer listened to the radio and teased his brother-in-law, whose mother defended him.

Henry grew more dignified as his house and the world about him descended into chaos. He kept his shoes in neat rows in his closet, each shoe with its shoe tree correctly in place. His shirts were boiled, his hats were blocked, his suits were darkly gray, his shoes were black, and his spats were clean. The women in his house dressed in wrappers and the other men went about in trousers and sleeveless undershirts.

When he went out in the evening, Henry went alone. On those occasions when he was obliged to bring a woman companion, he escorted his mother-in-law, whose Prussian reserve must have been the perfect complement to his Middle Eastern aplomb. Mostly he lived his public life. At home he put on his dressing gown and attempted to bring order to his house, always speaking quietly, working through diplomatic channels. He bore the great burden of his family as if he had spent his whole life preparing for it. He supported them all. He is not known to have complained. When I read the Book of Job, I thought of Henry.

Once, as far as I know, Henry permitted himself a trip across America by train. He stopped off in Texas to visit with us. It was summer. The sun was blinding. The heat was humming in the air. There was no one in the streets when Henry arrived. He wore a hat, a dark-gray suit, and spats. The pince-nez was on his nose. He instructed the driver to carry his luggage into our house. I think he had tea with us. It was made with a bag rather than being served from a samovar, as was his pleasure. He did not stay long. A few days after he had gone one of the Mexican kids who lived next door to us said that he had seen my uncle Henry and that he had looked like a king.

PHILLIP

Most of the witticisms attributed to my uncle Phillip are probably apocryphal. He is reputed to have said, in response to his wife's announcement that a watch would be a fitting bar mitzvah gift for his son, He wants a watch? Tell him to go by the window and watch.

When his son, then a medical student, brought home a Gentile girl to meet his parents, Phillip is said to have addressed the boy as Tom, a subtle pun on a Hebrew word for wrong thinking. The young woman, confused at hearing her beau called by an unfamiliar name, asked my uncle, Do you always call him Tom?

Only when he's with you.

Phillip and his tiny wife lived with constant barbs and teasing. As a child visiting in the house of my great uncle and aunt, I never knew whether to laugh at their teasing of each other. Politeness told me then to respond to their repartee with solemnity. I realize now that they were on-stage for their visitors, attempting to amuse. How disappointed they must have been at my lack of response!

Uncle Phillip was exactly the size and shape of a barrel. He had a ferocious black-and-gray beard, a little beak for a nose, and a black, shiny yarmulke on the back of his head.

His wife was about the size of an eight-year-old child and half the weight. She was very wizened and there was a large brown birthmark on the side of her face near her mouth, but because she was so tiny and had such a soft and mellifluously husky voice, children loved to be with her.

My father said Phillip was a yeshiva bucher, which is not exactly correct, for Phillip was not a student in a yeshiva, not at his advanced age. He did, however, live directly across the street from an Orthodox synagogue, where he spent all his days in prayer and discussion. How he came to live that way is rather curious.

Uncle Phillip was a junk dealer. That is, he was in the scrap metal and scrap-whatever-else business. If his wit was sharp, his business acumen was sharper. One does not rise from junk dealer to proprietor of a scrap metal business through miscalculation or lack of bargaining ability. Uncle Phillip was a very shrewd businessman. Everyone said so, even those who found his bickering wit irritating, even those who thought he carried his orthodoxy a bit too far for America, ordering his elder son out of the house for attending medical school classes on the Sabbath.

Despite his idiosyncracies, Phillip was on his way to becoming a millionaire. His business expanded. He took relatives into the business. He had a building, buildings. One day, at the height of his prosperity and promise, Uncle Phillip sat down in his office to take stock. He examined his needs and his responsibilities. After a time of consideration, he left his office and went to shul. It was too early for evening prayers. Perhaps he went to think about his life, to ask for guidance. Perhaps he had made an appointment with someone to debate a fine point of the Law. He didn't say. He went to shul and he stayed in shul. He never went back to his business.

Some years later Uncle Phillip's elder son started a clinic. It was long before medicare or medicaid or the widespread use of health insurance. The idea was to provide medical care for poor and lower-middle-class people. They paid a small sum each month. If they became ill, they were treated at the clinic. No matter how much care they required, the small monthly fee was all they paid. For his troubles Uncle Phillip's son was thrown out of the American Medical Association. He became a pariah in his own profession, perhaps to please his father.

Jews and interests have a strange history. If nothing else distinguished Jews from other people, their relationship to the normal human interests of survival and property would still make them unique. Historically a Jew and his money are soon parted. There have been some exceptions, but for a people in its fifty-eighth century even the duration of the Rothschild fortune seems brief. The connection between money and power is more complex than popular wisdom would have it. For Jews at least, riches have never guaranteed more than the comforts of the moment. Nothing has lasted for Jews but Judaism.

Historians have a passion for noting exceptions, so that the world seems to have been the work of great men. Popular histories, following an ancient tradition, show almost no interest in the quotidian life. In that view, Jews have been patriarchs, prophets, kings, philosophers, financiers, and advisors to kings. The true economic history of Jews presents quite a different picture. The patriarch was a nomad. The Jews of Egypt before Moses were slaves. During the existence of the first Jewish state in the promised land Jews lived mainly as small farmers, craftsmen, and herdsmen. A king was chosen, one suspects, primarily for defensive reasons. The Book of Kings is not a long book, for the kings of Israel did not have a very long reign or a very happy one. The Israelites spent much of their time as a conquered people, and conquered peoples are not rich.

The second stage of Jewish history is two thousand years of exile. For the most part, exiles do not live well. Maimonides advised Jews not to sell land to buy a house or to sell a house to buy some moveable object. It was good advice, but it was not very useful for a people who were often prohibited from owning land and sometimes forced to live in walled ghettos.

Exile, by its very nature, gives rise to some occupations. Wanderers learn various languages: The Jews became interpreters, traders, and money changers. Even being a pariah can lead to work, albeit work that no one else wants to do. Jews became tanners and moneylenders. Christians were prohibited from lending money at interest, so they gave the work to Jews and then levied heavy taxes on the Jews. It was an excellent system: The prince got the money and the Jews got the enmity. If the prince needed more money, he increased the taxes on the Jews, who in turn had to increase interest rates to pay the taxes.

In Eastern Europe Jews lived in abysmal poverty in the villages and in ghettos in the towns and cities. Jews did fairly well in Germany and France through the eleventh century. They did very well in the late fourteenth and almost all of the fifteenth century in Spain. From the end of the twelfth century on, Jews were at one time or another expelled from almost every country in Western Europe. Many settled in Eastern Europe during the early expulsions, only to suffer pogroms, all of which were terrible, but none so terrible as Chmielnitzki's massacre of the Polish Jews in 1648 and 1649.

The Crusades produced massacres of Jews. The Inquisition produced the torture, murder, and finally the expulsion of the Spanish and Portuguese Jews. The czar expelled thirty thousand Jews from Moscow in 1891. Slowly the lives of European Jews improved. Napoleon was helpful to Jews in achieving their civil rights in France. Disraeli, although a convert, was important to English Jews. Holland had been a refuge for centuries. Some Jews had gone to the Americas, although the great wave of emigration did not begin until the end of the nineteenth century. The home of Jews in Western Europe—the place where they flourished, living with the security of citizens, advisors, and veterans of the great war—was Germany. By the middle of this century all of that was over in Germany and most of Europe. Only England, France, and the Soviet Union now have significant Jewish populations.

It is a woeful history, but not a history only of woe. Nor are Jews the only people with a history of troubles. Most of Europe was destroyed by World War II: The Russians lost twenty million, Germany brought destruction on itself, Warsaw was leveled. British, French, and American losses were heavy in both world wars. Europe had its Hundred Years War and the United States endured a terrible civil war. Almost all the native population of the Americas has been wiped out. Biafra, Bangladesh, the famines of Africa, the decimation of Southeast Asia. The list of tragedies is a description of the history of man.

We can bear the list, the names and numbers, the familiar adjectives, but to have known a hundred families or even ten families that were destroyed might be maddening. The special case of the Jews is that virtually every Jew has been touched by murder in this generation, or the last, or the one before that.

If the history of Jews were limited to woes, it might be unbearable. Fortunately history may also be measured positively, according to the works of poets, the ideas of philosophers, and the lives of decent people. The positive history of Jews is as long and as extraordinary as the history of miseries. Suffering and philosophy, poverty and poetry, exile and community, tears and mercy are all intertwined in Jewish history. Jews have been rich and Jews have been poor. Only power, of all human situations, is unknown to Jews.

Following on that history, which is known in more or less detail by every Jew, a definition of Jewish interests cannot be easily made or agreed upon. There are five main groups of definitions of Jewish interests and five thousand distinct definitions within each of those large groups. One definition belongs to the ghetto and the shtetl; it suggests that Jews do best to keep to themselves, to engage in commerce with Gentiles, but to have no other intercourse with them. The Ḥasidim of Eastern Europe lived that way.

Zionists in all their forms hold that Jewish interests can only be served by a return to the homeland, where, many Zionists still believe, a nation can be created that will surpass all others in justice and peacefulness and mercy, a nation of love and culture. Others hold that a Jewish state must be far more practical if it is to survive.* Both kinds of Zionists—all kinds of Zionists—agree that a people without a

---

* After World War II a new kind of Zionist—the survivor at all costs—was born. For those Jews the almost continuous war against Israel had led to the abandoning of Jewish ethics, which are real, in favor of Jewish might, which is transitory at best.

The following dinner table conversation is illustrative of the ethical confusion of one who comes to accept killing as ordinary. It took place shortly after the Yom Kippur War. A colonel in Israeli intelligence described his willingness to be dropped by parachute into the Soviet Union to fight in a resistance movement in the event of a Soviet attempt to destroy the Jewish population. His wife, a biochemist, then said that she was working in chemical and biological warfare, developing weapons.

But you would never use them, I said.

If there were another war and it was going against us, I would use them. Yes.

But those kinds of weapons kill old people and children first.

She responded with a shrug.

home will always be a pariah, and they find that role both
dangerous and ignominious.

Throughout much of recent history—for the last two centuries at the very least—there have been Jews who believed
that their interests were best served by assimilation, that is,
the best that Jews could hope to do for themselves was to
stop being Jews. Evangelists of all religious denominations
have been willing to help Jews in their pursuit of that interest. Martin Luther, who professed to admire Jews for refusing to become Roman Catholics, expected Jews to convert
to his version of Christianity as soon as it was available to
them. When they did not, he argued that they should all be
exiled or killed.

Universalism, which came about with the Jewish Enlightenment, or Haskalah, and fought some fierce battles with
tradition, has a base in rationalism. The universalists were
the inheritors of the Haskalah, for once Jews had moved
into the world they could begin to understand how Jewish
ethics fit the Diaspora. As universalists, Jews came to understand that what was good for the rest of the world was also
good for the Jews. Peace, mercy, and social justice are the
interests of the universalists.

Each of the definitions of Jewish interests of the past has
in common with all the others the ethical and historical
basis of Judaism. Whatever the subtle differences in interpretation of the yoke of the Law, the ethical basis of the
Law remained. Judaism was the first ethical religion, the
first ethical civilization, and so it remains, even to the as-
similationists, who are willing to give up everything but the
ethics of their fathers.

The new definition of Jewish interests put forward by the
Jewish neoconservative movement in America and by the
rightist parties in Israel differs from all previous definitions
in that it pursues interests according to Darwinian princi-

ples. The new definition asks, "If I am not for myself, who
will be for me?" It fails to ask the second part of Hillel's
aphoristic question, "And being for myself, what am I?"

The new definition of Jewish interests belongs to an arrogant people. How can it belong to a small and humble
people? The new definition belongs to a selfish people. How
can it belong to a people who have been instructed to be
"a light to the nations"? The new definition belongs to a people of unlimited power and no history. How can it belong
to a people who remember that they were "sojourners in
Egypt"? One can understand how Jews could fear the outside world or wish for a homeland or wish to disappear
safely into another culture or seek the good life for all so
that they might enjoy it as well. The new definition has the
chill of loneliness about it. The expressions of it are sometimes grasping, sometimes combative, sometimes vengeful.

Milton Himmelfarb: "If we learn from our experience
with black leaders, we will not do favors for Hispanic
leaders."

Elliott Abrams: "Jews are not so secure that we can afford
to vote against our interests out of sentimental attach-
ments."

Norman Podhoretz: "Money, I now saw . . . was important: it was better to be rich than to be poor. Power, I now
saw . . . was desirable: it was better to give orders than to
take them."

Irving Kristol: "A nation whose politics revolves around
such issues as day-care centers or school lunches . . . is a
nation whose politics is squalid, mean-spirited, debasing."

Midge Decter on why homosexuals should not be tolerated: "The freedom to rise, it would seem, is also very much
the freedom to sink . . . In accepting the [Gay Lib] movement's terms, heterosexuals have only raised to a nearly in-
tolerable height the costs of the homosexual's flight from
normality. Faced with the accelerating round of drugs, S-M,

and suicide, can either the movement or its heterosexual sympathizers imagine that they have done anyone a kindness?"

Perhaps this new, merciless ethic has no connection at all with traditional Jewish ethics; perhaps the neoconservatives are the first pragmatic Jews. If so, the usefulness of ethics has been outrun by the speed of society, leaving behind any hope of freedom, justice, security, or peace. But even if the neoconservatives imagine a jungle drawn by Adam Smith and Charles Darwin and want nothing more than to survive at any cost, their ethics would be impractical. One need only reverse the roles of Jews and Gentiles for a moment to understand the folly of neoconservative thinking.

In the Diaspora Jews can never hope to be more than a small minority. Israel, for all its spartan successes, will never be more than a speck among nations. If the majority chooses to adopt the ethics of the Jewish neoconservatives, the future holds a grim promise. Midge Decter's attack on homosexuals as sadistic, masochistic, brutalized, suicidal, secretive, abnormal, and not really fit to live among other humans bears more than a slight similarity to the charges that have been made against Jews. If Milton Himmelfarb were not a Jew, one would expect his statement about blacks and Hispanics to include the third minority in America, the Jews.

The neoconservatives have forgotten who they are. They have fame, they are close to power as advisors to powerful men, and they remind their audiences that Jews are rich. They do not seem to recall that Jews are few. All of them are teachers or writers, men and women who are comfortable with adulation, at ease with the power of teachers over their students and of editors over writers. Men come in limousines and private planes to seek their wisdom.

Jeremiah described the difference between their position and that of Jewish ethics: "Thus saith the Lord: Let not the

wise man glory in his wisdom, neither let the mighty man
glory in his might, let not the rich man glory in his riches;
but let him that glorieth glory in this, that he under-
standeth, and knoweth Me, that I am the Lord who exercise
mercy, justice, and righteousness, in the earth." (Jer. 9:23)

The ethics of Jeremiah were not born in an ivory tower.
If any man knew the ways of the world and the abuses of
power, it was Jeremiah. The life of a prophet was a perilous
one: If he delivered bad news and it came true, he suffered
along with the rest of the people; if he delivered bad news
and it did not come true, he might be killed or exiled as a
false prophet. Jeremiah's father was sent into exile by King
Solomon; the prophet learned early on what a man might
endure if he disagreed with the powerful. Jeremiah himself
lived through Israel's defeats by the Babylonians and As-
syrians. He died in exile in Egypt. He was tried for treason.
He endured beatings, curses, prison. His works were shred-
ded and burned. He was thrown into a well and left to die.
Treachery, defeat, destruction, murder, corruption, and oppression were all well known to him. Yet he urged Jews to
seek the ethical life.

One does not expect a movement of editors and teachers
to have either the poetry or the vision or even the worldli-
ness of Jeremiah, nor does one expect such a movement to
have the temerity to preach loudly against the ethics that
have sustained a people for more than three thousand years.

The neoconservatives might argue that they have a
different message precisely because they have not suffered
in their own lives. They are the Jews who attended secular
universities, gaining prestige and financial security. They
are the Jews who send their children to secular universities
and see them move into greater spheres of prosperity and
security. They have come through the Judaism of Michael
Gold and Henry Roth and Philip Roth. They have come

through the Judaism of Abraham Cahan and Clara Lemlich and the ILGWU and Irving Howe. They have come through the Ku Klux Klan and Gerald L. K. Smith and restrictions and quotas. They have come through sweatshops and tenements and the depression and Brooklyn and the Bronx. They have made it. Jews worked in tanneries and collected dog dung and lived in ghettos, but that was a long time ago. This is America and these are good times for Jews in America. According to a recent poll concocted by Yankelovich, Skelly and White, Inc., only a third of all Americans are anti-Semitic. Many of the richest Jews in America made their fortunes in real estate; Jews have come a long way since the centuries when they were not permitted to own land.

A small, humble people now belong to the most powerful nation on earth. Use power! cries Norman Podhoretz. Build hydrogen bombs, nuclear submarines. Become ever more powerful. Only power can save America and only America can save the Jews.

The contradictions of human behavior are apparently endless in their variety. The many poor, often with little to maintain them but hope, hungry for bread, ill-clothed, would seem ready for the law of the jungle. As Marx said, What have they to lose? But the poor Jews of this world, the few, from the Hebrew prophets on, have seen their salvation in justice and mercy. Jeremiah, writing in a time before the promise of heaven had become the carrot of religion, living in the nadir of his nation, asks for mercy, justice, and righteousness.

Now the Jews are rich, according to the neoconservatives. It would seem the time for generosity. Surely it would not hurt the few rich to share what they have with the many poor, if not for ethical reasons then for the sake of peace and domestic tranquility. Yet the new Jews of the right support a president whose tax policy gives fifty times as much relief to the rich as to the poor, and whose social policy does not shrink from taking food from the mouths of children. Big Eddie gave to get what he wanted. He has been surpassed by those who want to keep what they have while getting more. The risk for Jews who adopt that philosophy is that they may become "a light to the nations."

4. 47th Street Photo

In New York conspicuous consumption means buying retail. Whatever has not "fallen off a truck" or cannot be bought from the manufacturer or the wholesaler must be bought at a discount store at least one flight up. Arabs and Texans buy retail in New York. All New Yorkers buy wholesale and know that they are sometimes getting shoddy merchandise and very often paying as much or more than they might pay in an ordinary store for sale goods. But it is a crowded city. Recreation is limited and expensive. One must be more than a spectator at sports; for his health's sake a person should participate.

Buying wholesale may have begun on the Lower East Side, but the sport has spread to every section of the city, to every race, religion, and economic class. In summer the streets of midtown Manhattan look like ancient bazaars set between rows of modern skyscrapers. In winter the most prosperously outfitted men and women may be seen struggling down the street, a huge unwrapped carton banging at the knee.

When it came time for me to buy a portable radio, I did
not want to behave like a fool or a stranger. For the sake of
my health, and to avoid Veblen's curse, I asked where I
might buy wholesale.

47th Street Photo is better than wholesale, said an academic. All the people on the faculty go there.

47th Street Photo is the place, said an executive. All the
businessmen go there.

No fool, I set out for 47th Street Photo. On the way I met
an acquaintance, an Englishman, who asked where I was
going. He said he knew the place and offered to accompany
me. We climbed the narrow stairs to the second floor, two
middle-aged gentlemen in Brooks Brothers trench coats (retail). The stairwell was dirty, the walls were unwashed, unpainted, unclean. Crudely lettered signs were posted on the
walls and at the top of the stairs. Great arrows of black on
fluorescent red backgrounds pointed the way.

A long time ago, in Texas, a shrewd retailer explained to
me that he always sold his merchandise with ugly signs and
crude hand-lettered advertisements. If you put a fancy face
on it, he said, people will think it's expensive. The cruder it
looks, the bigger the bargain. The price is less important
than the impression.

We entered a room so ugly that it promised better than
wholesale. There were shelves of raw wood, ancient display
cases with merchandise and old wrapping paper piled inside. The L-shaped sales area was crowded, hot, chaotic,
posted with more crudely lettered signs, reeking of sweat
and rot in the walls. People shouted and pushed. They
clamored for the bargains, which were kept somewhere
behind the carelessly constructed wall that hid the rest of
the room, or rooms, from the customers.

We pushed our way toward the counter where radios
were sold. As we neared it, now sweating like everyone else
in the salesroom, I saw that the salesmen were all young

Ḥasidic Jews. A fat boy in his twenties—his white shirt smudged; his fly partly unzipped below his bulging belly; his spotty, untrimmed beard curling with sweat—waited on the customer next to me. When my turn came, he said, Well?

I want an AM-FM portable radio, one that sounds reasonably good.

You want ten dollars? a hundred dollars? what?

Somewhere in the middle. Fifty.

He thrust a catalogue in front of me, opened it to the pages devoted to portable radios, and said, When you know, you'll tell me.

The Ḥasidim have given up ritual bathing, I thought, for I could smell him from across the counter. He stank of the gruel of sweat and detritus that collects in the creases of the body and sours. His clothes stank. His eyeglasses were smudged. His hands were pale and dirty. The bitten fingernails were blackened in the ridges between the ends of the fingernails and the bulbs of unrestrained fingertips.

He went on to another customer. I could not think of the radio, only of him, of this Jew who had presented himself to me. I chose a radio from the catalogue and waited for the salesman to return. Another came in his stead, younger and slim, with a soft reddish beard, a boy's beard of thinnest hair growing in patches and streaks down the sides of his face. We stared at each other for a moment, as if to compare our lives. I, too, wear a beard, a curly Jewish beard, once black, now turning gray.

He knew what I was thinking.

Well, what? he said. He did not hide his irritation at my examination of him.

This one, please. I pointed to a radio in the catalogue.

Not in stock. What else?

I'll need a moment.

Take all day.

He spoke with a heavy accent. While he waited for me to choose another radio, he spoke in Yiddish with the boy whose fly was partly unzipped. They complained to each other about a third person who screamed all day.

The salesman with the reddish beard returned to where I was standing. Ye-e-s? he said.

I pointed to another radio.

A wonderful choice, he said. Then he turned toward one of the entrances to the back rooms and shouted, Shloim, get me a G634K.

We waited, staring at each other. Hostility grew between us. He saw in my eyes what the *Ostjuden* had seen in the eyes of the German Jews. He could dance, he could fly, he could tell stories of the Baal Shem Tov that even Martin Buber did not know. How dare I look at him with scathing eyes!

The radio came. I inspected it and said I would buy it. He gave me a sales slip.

You'll pay the cashier; she'll give you the radio.

The boy and I continued to stare at each other. The Englishman tugged at my coat. We went across the room to the cashier's desk. The cash register was old, blackened where the gilt had rubbed away. The cashier was a woman of perhaps thirty years. Her eyes were large and dark, a history of the Jews. They gleamed as Esther's eyes must have gleamed. They had the promise of Esther's eyes and the fidelity of Ruth's eyes. They were not sorrowful eyes, but they had known sorrow.

I gave her the money. She gave me the package. We did not speak. She told me that she knew what I was thinking and that she had known similar thoughts. She smiled. It was not a real smile. It seemed to belong to a prisoner.

On the street I asked my acquaintance, Is it always like that?

Oh, close to Christmas it's far more hectic.

We walked a few blocks without speaking. There was a light rain falling. I gathered my collar closer to my neck. The trench coat was so different from the attire of the Ḥasidim!

It's difficult to be in a place like that, I said. That first one who waited on us.

Yes, he wasn't a very attractive fellow.

I'm so put off by them. I have to keep reminding myself that we're brothers.

You're not very much like them, you know.

For some reason the mark of tefillin seemed to be there again under my tweed jacket and Brooks Brothers trench coat. I heard the sounds of the kaddish, of the rhythmic praise, of the conjunctions piling up, of the four syllables repeated, of the changing words. Then I heard the harsh voices of the old men on Sabbath mornings loudly singing "Ein Ke-Elohenu." How I smiled when I sang with them! How happy I was to be one of them!

We walked north in the rain. The streets of Manhattan were thick with people at the noon hour. Few were Englishmen; many were Jews.

Shame.

According to biblical scholars, the idea was borrowed from the Gilgamesh epic. Perhaps that is so, but the simple shame of Eden has grown to a great and complex edifice in the hands of Western civilization. The dual purposes of shame are not always served; most especially, they cannot both be served when, as in the case of Jews, they can be in opposition. If juridical shame leads one to obey the Law in all its 613 daily details, he will be different from others, from the majority, who do not dress and act according to the Law. Then he will feel the shame of disapproval. That is the burden of a small people in a large world. Which shame shall a man bear?

To resolve the problem of shame in a large world one retreats to a small world, to a self-imposed ghetto or to a homogeneous nation, there to look out upon the larger world with disdain while obeying the Law. If one remains in the larger world, a resolution may be attempted by assimilation, but assimilation necessitates disdaining the Law in at least some of its aspects.

Zion, or a Zion in the mind, pleases some Jews, but others believe Zion is but a partial answer, for it is small and it suffers the disapproval of nations. Some who wish to remain in the larger world promote an exceeding pluralism, a society of molecules in which none is large enough to induce the shame of smallness in others. Unfortunately, a society of molecules, one that does not know disapproval for religious, racial, or ethnic reasons, cannot happen. Every man belongs to many categories, and men form ranks of those larger categories to promote their political, social, and economic ends. The shame of small peoples cannot be resolved—if the laws of the people make them distinct—unless tolerance becomes universal and so secure that the smallest group may come to accept it.

The unfortunate part about shame is that one is as likely to feel it when it is undeserved as when it is deserved; a person or a nation may feel deserved and undeserved shame alternately or simultaneously; and in a complex, confusing world a person may be uncertain about whether to feel shame or not.

Jewish shame begins in Eden. Perhaps. We could ask with Rashi, What do you mean, they didn't know they were naked? Even a blind man knows when he's naked! Shame comes from breaking the Law, not from nakedness. Shame truly began in the desert after the Law was given. It is conceivable that the Jews, having the first ethical religion, were the first to truly know the shame of breaking the Law. If that is so, we have the longest experience with awe of the

Lawgiver, shame at breaking the Law, and guilt over our misbehavior. But we are not alone in suffering that kind of shame. All people of all religions based on Judaism know the same kind. It could even be argued that shame is not unknown in any human society, for tribal taboos as well as written laws may bring about shame.

Shame at being a Jew must have begun in Egypt during the first exile. It is the shame that comes of disapproval, the shame of outcasts, slaves, minorities, of anyone who deviates willingly or unwillingly from the norm, no matter what the norm. The one who deviates may be far above the norm, as in the case of a studious, talented boy raised among thugs, but he will suffer the shame of disapproval for his deviation. The studious boy may leave the society of thugs for a society that approves of him. The Jew remains in the world.

Perhaps one of the reasons why the Jews were made to wander so many years in the desert was to overcome the shame of slaves. When the Talmud says "the shameless man's ancestors never stood at Sinai," it refers to shame at disobeying the Law, not to shame at being a Jew. Nor do the prophets deal with any shame but the shame of the sinner, for men were not punished by the disapproval of men, according to the prophets, they were punished by divine disapproval.

Shame at being a Jew is a creation of the Diaspora. Once dispersed, Jews had no hope of attaining power or even of defending themselves as a people: They could only choose between living with the disapproval of the majority and disappearance into the majority. The shame learned at Sinai was more to be feared. Awe of God was greater than awe of man. The Jews chose disapproval. If they knew that shame would follow on that disapproval, they did not speak of it. Perhaps it would have made their decision more difficult; perhaps their awe of God was so great that they never re-

ally considered the alternative. If what we read of such
Jewish martyrs as Akiva, Ḥanina, Jesus, and all those who
fought at Masada is true, awe of God created men for
whom the disapproval of men, even when it was expressed
in the form of torture and murder, paled before the disapproval of God.

In 1215 the yellow-badge decree of the Fourth Lateran
Council institutionalized the disapproval of men. For almost
seven hundred years the Jews of Europe lived with a yellow
badge or a yellow hat. Cursed moneylenders, ghetto dwellers, strangers, killers of Christ, the cause of plagues, scum
one day and dangerously shrewd the next—they were slaughtered, tortured, robbed, raped, banished, and banished again
from country after country. Their only respite came in the
aftermath of the French Revolution. Always and everywhere, for twenty-five generations, they were forced to make
the choice between shame before God and shame before
man.

Popular books by Jews have attempted to turn the Jew-
badge into a badge of courage. They tell of the enlightened
Gentiles who admired Jews for wearing the badge rather
than giving up their religion. They tell of the strength of the
Chosen People through all those centuries of life as a
pariah. In these popular histories Jews are depicted as
superhuman. They are books of piety and defiance, never of
shame.

Is it possible that Jews could rise completely above the
pain of disapproval that we call shame? Could that have
happened in generation after generation, century after century? The literature of the Spanish Inquisition and, even before that, of the advice to the Jews of Morocco by Maimonides indicates that Jews were affected by disapproval in
more than merely economic ways. He tells the Jews of Morocco to emigrate, for it is a sin to remain among those who

deny God even if "they do not force anyone to do as they do." He knows the power of disapproval.

The fifteenth-century Spaniard Judah ben Jacob Hayyat tells of a hundred people aboard a ship who apostacized in a single day. He recounts his own miseries but ends with his survival as a Jew. The purpose of a martyrology is not to glorify the suicide or murder or torture of the martyr, but to shore up the will of the faithful to endure the disapproval of man, to add the approval of man to the approval of God, to shame men into remaining faithful. For the same reason all religions attack the apostate as the worst of sinners. It was not for their own pride that the Sephardim called the converts *marranos* (swine) but to fight shame with shame.

To live with a history of martyrs, or even in a time of martyrs, gives courage to a people; by examples of faith they gain the force of opposition. One becomes afraid not to have courage, for the courage of martyrs multiplies the shame of cowards. To live in a ghetto and wear a ridiculous yellow hat upon leaving the ghetto, to suffer taunts and scorn, to be a pariah and the child of pariahs, to have no future but to be the parent of pariahs does not inspire noble sentiments. To live for seven centuries as an object of hatred and disgust does not leave a people without questions about itself.

The shame of disapproval results in rhinoplasty and changed surnames, in psychological disappearance and new ethics. Fear can make a man brazen. Shame over oneself has no result but cowering and the wish to be someone else. The shamed man dreams of awakening one morning in the body of another person to live another person's life. In real life he gives himself away in parts, trading more and more until he has either found some accommodation with shame or he has disappeared entirely.

The shame of Jews at being Jews in America differs from

everything we have known in the past. We have integrated.
Paul Newman and Sandy Koufax are Jews. Jews can be
elected to public office. The shame now has to do with ethics. Both history and the Law led Jews to sit on the left side
of the aisle, to strive for social justice, to trust in equality.
Now those long-held ethical principles have been converted
by the Jewish neoconservatives into a new Jew-badge. They
have made Jewish ethics reek of sweatshops and communal
toilets, of bargaining in the streets and holding union meetings in the hallways and cellars. When Norman Podhoretz
attacks Irving Howe for equating Judaism and socialism in
World of Our Fathers, it is not the yeshiva bucher from
Brooklyn who is speaking but the advisor to Ronald Reagan
who underwent "conversions" at Columbia and Cambridge.

The new Jew-badge is not a yellow star or a yellow hat. It
is a picture of Karl Marx or Leon Trotsky or Abraham
Cahan or Emma Goldman or the Hollywood Ten or Samuel
Gompers. The essence of Judaism has become the badge
of shame at being a Jew in the minds of those who would
now avoid the disapproval of the majority by escaping into
the love of money and power and forgetting the attributes
of mercy and loving-kindness that gave Jews to believe man
was indeed created in the image of God.

In the neoconservatives the two kinds of shame face each
other squarely, as always in Jewish history, and shame before the disapproval of man has won out: The leaders of the
neoconservative movement do not want to appear in the
world as foolish old Jews of the ghetto, crying out for social
justice for all, social justice so pervasive that it includes the
Jew. Nor do they believe mercy and social justice must be
brought about through the law of the land. They are for the
strong. They are for the efficiency of the market in all
things, for they identify with the strong. Shame for them is
to be a poor and humble people and to behave accordingly.

At the heart of their choice, they say, is an abiding belief in the market efficiencies of capitalism. They have whole-heartedly embraced the theory of the invisible hand. It is an interesting theory and very much to the benefit of some, but it is not a theory that can be made compatible with Juda-ism. The invisible hand devolves from the antinomian ideas of Saul of Tarsus; Jewish ethics devolve from the visible hand of the Law.

Perhaps the neoconservatives have found the way to end the shame of disapproval that Jews have known for so many centuries. Perhaps Irving Kristol or Sidney Hook could go to 47th Street Photo without feeling that the face of the man across the counter was his face and that as one is the face of a pariah so is the other. It is possible. But we have lived for a long time with the ethics of the visible hand. We have worked for a long time to make those ethics universal so that we might survive and live without either kind of shame. Perhaps a world of universal tolerance and mercy is not possible and the notion of earning the coming of the Messiah through the creation by man of a messianic period is a foolish dream. If so, the neoconservatives have an an-swer, but it is not the answer of those who inherited the leg-acy of Sinai, for it is a shameless answer, and Jews are not without shame.

5. The Basketball Player of Lublin

They ate cockroaches.

You shouldn't say that about them.

It's true. My father was at the meeting with the sponsors. He said that the old man stood up in front of all the sponsors and told how the family ate cockroaches.

It's true?

It's true, dummy. They lived in a cave and ate cockroaches. God knows what else!

The family of six Polish refugees came to our town after the war. They were a uniformly ugly family. All of them had little eyes and lumpy noses and sickly, translucent skin. They wore other people's clothes. The father was very small. He seemed smaller inside the double-breasted suits and white shirts that had been hastily tailored to approximate his size. He had several hats, all of them softened with age and only slightly too large. The impression was of a man in extremely heavy clothing, struggling to move the weight of his sleeves, so tired by the burden of his hat that he sank into his collar.

The mother had two gold teeth.

All the children had dirty-blond hair and suspicious eyes. The boys wore short pants and the girls never took off their coats.

No one in the family spoke English. The mother and father made themselves understood in Yiddish, but the children were limited to Polish and only a few Yiddish words. We spoke to them with signs and grunts, and sometimes with less than gentle shoves. They were an irritation in the lives of the genteel Jewish children in our town. Soon they became a burden. The children tried to avoid the children and the parents gossipped about the parents. People began to ask how the family had avoided the concentration camps, why they had not gone to Israel. Maybe they weren't really Jews. We listened to the father daven to be certain that our suffering and sacrifice were, at least, for a Jewish family.

An old house next to the synagogue was rented by the sponsors to be a home for the refugee family. Furniture was donated; also pots and pans, incomplete sets of stainless steel knives, forks, and spoons; a stepladder with one missing step; and a vacuum cleaner that sputtered. The castoffs of a hundred houses were delivered to the refugees. They had more tables than chairs, more mattresses than beds. It was a sorry house made worse by the jumble of things thrown into it. Nothing matched but the house and its inner chaos and the people who inhabited the house.

No one was quite certain about employment for the father. The refugees had come from Lublin, or near Lublin, either from a farm or a small town surrounded by farms. The father said he was not a farmer, but when he was asked about his trade he had no trade. Was he a shopkeeper, a tailor, a presser, an ironmonger, a baker, a butcher, what?

Please tell us, the sponsors asked, what can you do? The father answered, as always, that he and his family had escaped the Nazis and the Polish cossacks, who were worse than the Nazis. They were glad to be in America. While hiding from the Nazis and the Polish collaborators, they had lived in caves and eaten anything that God provided, including insects.

A job was found for the father in a cleaning and dyeing plant. He was to press pants. He complained that the work was too hard and the hours were too long. He had lived in a cave and eaten insects. He was not a strong man. The owner of the plant reduced his hours.

The mother was invited to coffee klatches with the women of the community. Many of the older women of the community had also been refugees. They told her about the terrible crossing in steerage, the life-or-death inspection at Ellis Island, the strangeness of America. The mother admired their houses. She told them she needed draperies and a good mattress that would support her back. She asked for new pots and for a machine that would mix the dough for cakes and bread, and for a sewing machine so she could make dresses for her daughters.

One of the older women said, You know, it's not a picnic to be an immigrant. What we came over was not exactly first-class.

The mother said, We lived in a cave. We ate insects.

The women of the community shook their heads in wonder at her suffering. They asked her if she wanted a sewing machine with a buttonhole attachment or without.

With the money he earned from his job the father went to a car dealer, who was a member of the committee of sponsors, to buy a truck. The dealer took ten dollars for a down payment on a small van and told the refugee father to pay him the rest whenever he could—ten dollars a month,

five dollars a month, a dollar a month if that was all he
could afford. The refugee father asked him to fill the tank
with gasoline.

The younger children learned English quickly. The older
boy, who was sixteen, made very little progress. He was
moody. He had little tantrums. If someone pushed him, he
pushed back. The only thing that really interested him was
basketball. Every afternoon he came to the basketball court
in the community center to watch the other boys practice.
One afternoon he appeared in the gym dressed in a white,
sleeveless undershirt, a pair of swimming trunks, black
stockings with white clocks, and brown wing-tip shoes that
flopped at the heel.

An informal game was in progress when he arrived. No
one paid him much notice until he stepped onto the floor
and caught the ball. The players shouted at him or stood
with their hands on their hips, tapping their feet and making sour faces. One of the boys went to take the ball from
the refugee. He wrapped his arms around it, refusing to let
go. There was a struggle for the ball. The refugee lost his
footing on the polished floor. Both boys fell. They rolled
over each other on the hard floor, fighting for the ball,
fighting each other. Finally the refugee boy scrambled to
his feet and jumped away from the other boy. There was a
red floor burn on his forehead, his lip was bleeding, and he
shone with sweat. For a moment he looked at the other boys
on the floor, waiting for one of them to try to take the ball
from him, defying them. No one moved. No one spoke.

He tucked the ball under his arm and ran clumsily down
the floor to the farthest basket. Several times he had to stop
to regain his balance as his leather-soled shoes slipped on
the polished hardwood. When he was close to the basket, he
slid to a stop, composed himself, and threw the ball at the
hoop. It went over the backboard and hit the wall.

The ball bounced back toward him, but he made no attempt to retrieve it. He turned to face the other boys. Thick blood oozed out of the burn on his forehead. He addressed the two teams assembled before him.

Shit, he said.

As far as I know, he never learned to play basketball: He refused to dribble, no matter how many times he was told, no matter how many times the ball was taken from him. A few weeks after the basketball game his father drove the van up to their sorry house, dragging an old wooden trailer, like a giant chicken coop, behind it. All that day the father, the mother, and their four children carried their American possessions out of the house and into the trailer. Everything was moved into the trailer, piled there in no apparent order, as if it were meant for burning. When the house was empty, the six refugees loaded themselves into the van and drove away. I do not know where they went.

Some years ago a publicist from a Jewish fund-raising organization telephoned me to ask if I would be interested in a trip to Europe. He began the conversation with flattery. The organization he represented had just published a piece of mine on the front cover of its monthly bulletin. The piece, which had first been published on the Op-Ed page of the New York *Times* and then reprinted in Israel, was a letter to a Russian friend about the Yom Kippur War. He connected it somehow with the death camps of World War II, for that was the trip he wanted me to make. A group of young Jewish couples was going on a tour of death camps and I was to accompany them, interview them, observe their reactions, and then write about them for a magazine or newspaper.

It was not a good conversation. Flattery makes me uncomfortable; I do not know how to respond. Sponsored writing makes me more uncomfortable; I have always preferred to earn my living in some way other than writing so that necessity would not do violence to my work.

Your offer is very flattering, I said. Would you mind if I took a day or two to think it over?

He said he would telephone again in a week.

When we talked again, I told him there were some problems with the idea. What if the women, after visiting a death camp, spent the evening talking about fashion or looking for a hairdresser? What if the men—all young professionals, he had promised—left Dachau talking of the stock market?

Would that be important? he asked.

If it happened, I would write that it happened.

You would have to say that?

Not that necessarily. Whatever happened is what I would write. I'm giving you an example.

You wouldn't keep in mind what's good and what's bad to say?

Yes. I would say what's good for the Jews. That's what I'm telling you.

Then you wouldn't say that.

Aren't we the people of the Book? Isn't the Book the example to Jews?

Yes, yes, he said.

Then surely a Jewish organization would want a Jewish writer to tell the truth.

We spoke once more a day later. Upon reconsideration of the cost of sending a writer along, he said, it had been decided that there simply wasn't enough money in the budget, particularly without some guarantee of publication.

I do not know what the Holocaust means. I am not certain that anyone does. The word confuses me, for it means the consumption of everything in fire, as if there were a great accident, as if there might have been something natural about the disaster that befell our people. It was an assassination, a murder, an efficient slaughter, a bloody killing of children.

When I was a boy I worked in a research laboratory in a hospital. The doctor who supervised the laboratory was a strange man. He lived in darkness, an obstetrician who refused to deliver babies, a man without anger, as if it had been removed from him by some surgical process, a German. He was very large and very bald and he spoke with a heavy accent.

I asked if he was a Jew. He was not.

The doctor frightened me. Because of his age and his accent he had to have been in Germany during the war. I had visions of him performing experiments, working in the camps.

His wife told his assistant, who told me that the doctor had indeed worked in the camps.

Following his graduation from medical school and his residency in obstetrics, he was conscripted into the German Air Force. They had no use for obstetricians, so they made him a member of the flight crew of a bomber. He flew on the first raid over Poland in 1939. When he returned from the mission, he said he would not fly again for the Luftwaffe. He was sent to a concentration camp. From the last months of 1939 until the end of the war he practiced his specialty. He told his wife he had delivered thousands of babies, perhaps ten thousand. He delivered them alive, doing the best he could with the primitive equipment available to him. Then the babies starved or died in the gas chambers or on the ends of bayonets. Of all the thousands of babies who first breathed while he held them in his hands not one survived to leave the camps.

He lived in dark rooms wherever he went. He avoided the light. He did not wish to live a human life. Science interested him—biochemistry, endocrinology—but not the whole human being. Sometimes, when I passed his office and saw him sitting in the darkened room, a huge figure in his white coat, his desk dark but for a tiny circle of light, I wondered what he knew, what he had learned, whether he regretted his decision.

It occurs to me now, twenty-five years later, that he knew nothing, that he had learned nothing, that his grand gesture no longer held any interest for him. He had been to the unimaginable darkness. I thought of him when I read Tadeusz Borowski's book.* Had his work also become routine? normal? Had he descended that far? I think not. Borowski was a suicide at the age of thirty-one.

Then what had the doctor found out? Nothing. He had learned that men cannot see in the dark.

If it was a holocaust, how did the doctor survive? It was not everything, not everyone was consumed. One could almost understand a holocaust, a blind rage that consumed everything, a murderous madness. It is the order that is unfathomable, the selectivity, the rationality, the science, the routine, the efficiency.

It pains me to think it, but there is nothing new under the

---

* *This Way for the Gas, Ladies and Gentlemen, and Other Stories* (1967), a book of stories about the German death camps describing the quotidian nature of life for inmates who were not murdered. In perhaps the most chilling scene ever written about the camps, one of the inmates is playing soccer on a makeshift field when he sees a trainload of Jews arrive to begin the sorting process. He wonders which will become slave laborers and which will be sent directly to the gas chambers. He notes their arrival but then becomes involved in a play. A goal is scored. He looks out again at the platform beside the railroad tracks. Everyone is gone. In the time it took to score a goal a trainload of human beings had passed through the system of assassination.

sun, as the prophet said. Once in Egypt there was a slaughter of innocents, of the firstborn sons.*

We are careful not to think of the morality of that ancient slaughter. The commentary on it is almost gleeful, extending the number of those killed by broadening the definition to include two subcategories apparently overlooked by Scripture: 1) the head of the household if he had produced no sons; and 2) more than one son of the same woman if the sons were sired by different men. No questions are raised about that selective, efficient killing of innocents. Perhaps it happened too long ago, perhaps no one believes the Bible as literal truth. But why is such a terrible thing told if it is not true?

If we can live with that ancient mass slaughter and find good reasons for it, admire it, and teach it to our children, what does that portend for our eventual understanding of the Nazi death camps? Will the death of millions eventually become cold history? An example of some power, some philosophy, some theology? Perhaps some future generation will say it was a test of theodicy. Even now there are those who would make the murder of millions a tool, something of the useful history of man. A soupy drama for television has been made of the darkness, as if sentimentality were the bringer of light. Some people have said that there were no death camps, no ovens, no babies killed with bayonets, not literally, not exactly, not the way the Jews tell it.

The death camps will have their uses. Ambitious men use history like sausage makers: They employ the whole, wast-

---

* The Egyptians had once also decreed the death of newborn male children, but the decree was not carried out with divine efficiency—Moses survived. Moreover, Pharaoh decreed the death of all newborn males, including Egyptians, for his sorcerers did not know whether Pharaoh's undoing would be at the hands of a Hebrew or an Egyptian.

ing nothing; they are efficient. The anti-Semites will have
their uses and the Jews will have theirs.

Was Hannah Arendt right about the banality of evil?
Borowski would agree. I do not know what the obstetrician
would say; he looked back on darkness; he did not choose to
consider the moral qualities of man. Arendt strode into the
darkness to find out what was there. There is no sign in her
work that the darkness frightened her. But one wonders if
there were not some nights when the woman who so loved
rationality did not fear, even for a moment, that she had entered the time and place without light.

Do I propose some mystical notion of genocide? I am a
Jew; I cannot afford to think that any force greater than the
moral blindness of man makes beasts with human cunning.
Nor can I afford to think that God intercedes in the works
of man anymore. If He did, if He could, if the darkness was
His creation, what new system of morals can be invented to
account for His work? If He chose to permit the darkness,
what is not permitted? What shalt thou not do?

We are alone, chosen, and abandoned to think what we
will of the darkness.

Stories are made to explain the darkness to us, stories always of the Jewish doctor whose children love Mozart, of
poets, rabbis, loving women, sweet children. What of the
man whose fly was half open and whose body stank of old
sweat? What of the shrew, the nasty child, the fool, the beg-
gar, the farmer reeking of dung? Do we seek some creature
more perfect than human, some special man, so that man
can be mindful of him? Why is it so difficult to love the
family that lived in caves and ate insects?

The darkness spreads like ink spilled across history. It is
the evil that makes light of all other evils. Compared to the
murder of the Jews, what is slavery? what is poverty? what
is the murder of one man or ten? What suffering in daily life
is even deserving of consideration?

I do not understand the murder of the Jews of Europe, not the calm of it, not the scope of it, not the efficiency of it. The current American fascination with the history in detail of Nazi Germany nauseates me. I do not know why. I know why: because I am afraid of the dark.

The uses of darkness also frighten me. Rabbi Meir Kahane said, "Never again!" and acted like a madman. The State of Israel, flouting international law and convention, abducted a man, tried him in open court, sentenced him to death, and destroyed him as punishment for his administration of the darkness, for his moral blindness. Was there not some other way even for him, some way that might have slowed the spread of darkness? Now the new Jews of the right in America imply that after the murderous darkness the imperative of survival overwhelms all other questions.

They cannot be denied that conclusion. After the murder of innocents was the routine of men, fear of the darkness haunts all Jews. To be denied social and genetic immortality is the greatest crime that can be committed against a people. The answer to that kind of an attack must not be, as so many Jews have said, to finish Hitler's work ourselves. When Jews speak those warnings, they speak as theologians, insisting that Jews must not give up their belief in God because He did not answer them at Auschwitz.

But one could be a deist without being a Jew. One could believe in an interceding God without being a Jew. The problem is how to be a Jew after Auschwitz. If physical survival is all that is required to defeat the darkness, Jews would do best to convert now, to become Christians in the Christian world, Muslims in the Middle East, Buddhists in India, atheistic communists in the Soviet bloc countries. The Marranos made that choice in Spain, which is how they came to be called swine.

The Jewish neoconservatives advise survival by selfishness, the pursuit of Jewish interests through war and through abandoning the love of mercy.

There was no mercy in the camps, in what has been described as a war against the Jews.

If the darkness reaches out to the inheritors of the first ethical religion, what will become of them? What will become of the world? For three thousand years—through defeat and exile, torture, calumny, ridicule, and murder—the Jews have remained the people of the Book, proof that justice and mercy are stronger than the weaknesses of men. But there has never been a darkness like the darkness that fell over Europe; nothing so fearsome ever touched the earth. Even the destruction of Hiroshima and Nagasaki pales before the quotidian routine of killing.

The darkness spreads by fear: It urges men to think of themselves with their backs to the wall, living in a world without limits; it denies the utility of ethics and the value of mercy; it fosters the vision of man as a beast that can speak. The temptation to live in the darkness is enormous. Fear deceives a man into thinking he is bargaining for his life when he accepts the darkness as the only reality.

Jews cannot survive in the darkness, not as Jews. They may become something else, enjoying physical survival for a time at least, but embracing the darkness completes its work. All of history vanishes, all of ethics gives way to rationalization; a night beyond measurement descends.

A different response to darkness was agreed upon in the desert more than three thousand years ago. Who other than the Jew could be expected to understand that the war against the darkness must be fought with mercy and justice? Who other than the Jew could survive a nightmare no man could dream? If God looked for a strong opponent to put into the arena against the worst of the will of man, who could He find stronger than the Jew? For three thousand

years and more Jews have trained for the battle: in Jerusalem and Babylonia and Cordoba and Vilna and Berlin and
New York; in great temples and in schoolrooms no more
than shacks; in Rashi's vineyards and in the Baal Shem Tov's
bath; in sweatshops and on picket lines; in the legal battles
for civil rights and in tank battles for a piece of desert. The
Jew comes armed with history and ethics. He has learned
from the Talmud that cruelty to the stranger is a greater sin
than cruelty to another Jew. He has learned the value of
mercy by studying the Law and by experiencing the lack of
mercy in the world. He knows that as the cruelty of darkness seeks universal sway, the mercy of the Jew must be
universal. He knows that as the darkness reaches first for
the weakest, he must stand with the weak.

The rules of being a Jew have been the same for a hundred generations. Written exegesis of the rules fills a thousand volumes. The rules were challenged at Auschwitz as
never before. A movement to revise the ethics of Jews in
light of the recent past has naturally arisen, for Jews are not
angels; but Jews are an old people and curiously immutable.
If history provides any clues, the neoconservatives will return to the ancient ethics or Judaism will go on without
them.

When I was a boy I was told that the reason why there
were no musical instruments in the synagogue was that we
were mourning the destruction of the Temple in Jerusalem.
Christians could have organs in their churches, but Jews
would not have organs until the return to the homeland. It
was a great confusion to me. I did not know what Christians
were, nor did it ever occur to me that the Paul Whiteman
orchestra should be playing in the synagogue. I was six
years old and I thought my country was America and my
homeland was Illinois. Israel was an imaginary land, the setting for the Bible, a place as far away as it was long ago.

A fellow named Maynard who sat next to me in ḥeder explained who Christians were. Goyim.

I knew who goyim were. They didn't vote for Roosevelt, they mixed meat with milk, and they prayed to a man instead of to God. There were many, many more goyim than Jews, but not in our neighborhood.

Maynard, who was nine years old, although only in first-year ḥeder, had no information on Israel. As far as he knew, he was an American. He had an uncle who was with Patton and two cousins who were fighting the Japs in the Pacific. He showed me a trading card with a picture of a tank like the one his uncle drove.

There were no Zionists in my family, nor were there any Republicans. We were Americans and Democrats; our religion was Jewish. Our skin was white, but we were to be kind to people who were colored, because they had been slaves, just as Jews had been slaves in Egypt. One other class of people existed—the Irish. They were not Jews, but the Irish were also not included among the goyim. Al Horan was Irish and so was Marty O'Brien. The Irish were in the same category as Reform Jews; they didn't wear yarmulkes when they prayed, but they were for Roosevelt and against the Japs and Germans.

Consciousness of Israel did not come to our house until the war was over. It arrived in the form of bond drives and little blue cans with white lettering. Suddenly there seemed to be talk of little else. My mother and grandmother went to Hadassah meetings, my grandfather spoke of bonds for Israel in staggering amounts; more than enough to buy a house was being asked of all the co-chairmen of the latest bond drive.

Then, with even greater suddenness, Israel was a state and it was at war. We learned to sing "Adon Olam" as it was sung by the Haganah. There was a Jewish army. Jews were fighting against Arabs led by German officers. The

Jews were outgunned, outnumbered. They were in danger
of being destroyed. But the Jews were winning. It was like
a story out of the Bible re-enacted as a twentieth-century
fable. The stories said everyone fought: old men, women,
boys of twelve. I dreamed of running away to join the
Haganah.

Israel arrived as a romantic notion, dressed in tales of her-
oism, daring, and something called a kibbutz, a place where
perfect young people lived a perfect life of love, work,
brotherhood, and self-defense. One never heard the name of
the Jewish state without some stirring music imagined in
the background. Had God answered the prayers of Auschwitz by giving Israel back to the Jews?

My country, however, was not Israel. The Law was clear:
A Jew was to support the government of the country in
which he lived, even in war, even if in war he had to fight
against Jews who lived in an enemy country. The only exception was a government that asked Jews to renounce their
religion. But that law was written during the Diaspora. If a
boy was about to be bar mitzvah and Israel was the Jewish
state, even if he lived in America and was a Democrat and a
White Sox fan, did that boy owe his love to America or Israel? And if he tried to avoid the question by telling himself
that he loved both America and Israel, which did he love
more? What if America went to war against Israel?

We lived at the edge of town in the third house from the
beginning of a cornfield that reached to the horizon. My
friend was a giant dog, an immensely stupid German Shep-
herd registered under the name Duke of Kelev. The Duke
and I discussed philosophical questions in a secret place
hidden among the corn rows. Either it was his nature or our
discussion of violence affected him in an unfortunate way, I
do not know which; but the Duke turned killer. He killed

for sport: rabbits, cats, any kind of small animal. The dead animals were left on the milk stoop. They were never bloody. Apparently he killed by shaking the smaller animals until he broke their necks. Several times he picked up a rabbit in his jaws and demonstrated the method for me, then laid the twisted animal at my feet. I scolded him; I shouted at him; I beat him with a folded newspaper. Nothing could dissuade him. After a while I gave up. We put an advertisement in the local newspaper. A few days later someone came to take the Duke of Kelev. I was not unhappy; violence, even the violence of a dog, was unseemly.

In the same season a schoolmate called me a kike. We fought over the insult, two sweaty boys crying and punching each other in a school yard. Just as we were becoming too tired to continue the fight, he screamed and backed away. His face was smeared with blood. There was blood on my hands and my shirt. He fell over. Blood was running out of his face. It was only a broken nose that caused the bleeding, but I thought for a moment that I had killed him.

The pleasure of beating someone bloody confused me. The principal punished me, but my fellow students were lavish in their approval. A girl kissed me in the school yard. I looked in books for an answer. Human nature? What was the nature of humans, to be violent or loving? To be both? To have the capacity to be either? To be alternately peaceful and loving and violent and hating? I hit upon self-defense, discarded it as a lie, and took it up again as the only answer.

Violence dogged me all the early years of my life. I fought in the halls of a college dormitory, in bars, on the streets. On my very first day in the Air Force I fought with an ex-Marine until he lay unconscious on the barracks floor, and when the sergeant in charge of our flight came to the upper bay of the barracks to see what had happened, I was ready to fight with him, too.

Fighting had something to do with being a Jew, with the way Jews had not fought when the Germans came to take them to the death camps, and with the way Jews had fought when the Arabs came to kill them in Israel. I grew to admire the refugee family that had lived in caves and to question the courage of the doctor who had been so passive in the darkness, delivering babies instead of turning his scalpel against the closest German guard. When Bruno Bettelheim published his essay against the passivity of the Frank family, I wrote congratulations to him. Jews fought. Jews survived because they fought. If Jews did not fight, who would fight for them?

Life is simple for the young. Oppositions sit easily in them. A young man can love both war and peace. He can be both large and small. The world appears to him as a toy. A gentle woman and the birth of innocents teach a boy to look at the world through the eyes of a man. Peace belongs to men as war belongs to boys. Mercy rules a father's hand. Once, when our first son was ill, we did not have enough money to buy the medicine prescribed for him. That was my bar mitzvah. I understood how the world worked and why a poor and humble people, a nation in slavery, had been chosen. The pieces of Jewish ethics I had heard and read all my life fit into a system.

No man is smaller than one who cannot buy medicine for his child. I was not wretched or illiterate or filthy or lazy. I was broke. When the druggist told me the cost of the medicine, I said, I don't have it.

Get the money, you'll get the medicine.

He was a little old Jewish man with wisps of white hair on his head and a white mustache no more luxuriant.

There was an old fishing knife in the pocket of my jacket. Give it to me, I said, or I'll take it.

The old man smiled. His eyes closed and he nodded. What you mean, he said, is you really don't have it.

I have about half of it.

So why didn't you say so? He handed the bottle of medicine to me. I offered the money that was in my pocket.

Keep it. A sick boy should have a father with a few dollars in his pocket. When you'll have extra, you'll pay me.

How do you know I'll pay you?

He gave a lazy shrug. I know.

How do you know?

What is this? Twenty questions? Go home! He pointed to the door. Your boy is sick, your wife is worried. Go home!

The druggist was a Jew. He understood the difference between money and mercy. I think he delighted in giving lessons. Did he do it because he knew I was also a Jew? I think not; Jews do not believe that other Jews threaten druggists.

A believer in the invisible hand cannot behave like the old druggist; a return to the philosophy of John Calvin and Adam Smith leaves no room for mercy, because mercy interferes with nature. Man's mercy, in that view, may contradict the will of God, for God doesn't make men poor unless they deserve to be poor. How different from the visible hand! In Jewish Law man's mercy is not an interference with God's will, it *is* His will.

In a strangely convoluted argument against mercy, the Jewish neoconservatives say that the 1967 war in the Middle East led them to the pursuit of Jewish interests. They applaud Israel the strong, supporting the Begin government in its appropriation of Arab lands and in its killing retaliations. The 1967 war, they say, made them more aware of the Holocaust and taught them that Jews might be destroyed after all. The leap from the defense of Israel to the defense of the Haves against the Have-Nots seems to have no possible genesis but the sudden appearance in the world of a Jewish fist.

For two thousand years Jews relied upon the justice and

mercy of others for their existence. At any time, in any
country, the majority could have destroyed the Jews by
exile or assassination—and sometimes they did. With the establishment of the State of Israel, Jews became the dis-
pensers of mercy and justice instead of the recipients. It was
said that Jews could now hold up their heads, for they had
a homeland like other people; they were no longer wanderers.

Perhaps Jews became too much like other people. With
victory after victory, always against superior numbers, always against the combined forces of the Arab world, Israel
gave a sense of power to American Jews. Few Jews thought
of the Arab dead or of the Palestinians raising their generations as people without a country, duped by the other Arab
countries, defeated by the Jews, left with no way to shout
their existence but to fall from civilization to terrorism.

Israel, the imaginary power in the Middle East, serves as
an excuse for every new move to the right by American
Jews. The blacks spoke against Israel; therefore the Jews
will oppose busing and side with those who want to cut
health and welfare expenditures and rail against affirmative
action programs.

If Israel is the answer to the Holocaust, was Israel not to
be a different answer? Was Israel not conceived as the state
that would be a model for the world? Was Israel not a
dream of the rule of ethics, the home in the world, at last,
of justice and mercy? Even the Declaration of Indepen-
dence of the State of Israel, after taking into account the di-
sastrous slaughter in Europe and the need for a Jewish
homeland, promises that "the State of Israel . . . will be
based on the principles of liberty, justice, and peace as conceived by the prophets of Israel; will uphold the full social
and political equality of all its citizens . . ."

The Zionists who inherited the dream of Hess and Gordon and turned it into the realism of Ben-Gurion made a

Jewish response to the murder of the Jews by the Nazis; their response and that of the Jewish neoconservatives are virtually perfect opposites.

Under the Begin regime Israel has changed. It now demands the surrender of the Arabs, who demand the surrender of the Israelis. At the moment there is peace with Egypt and war with the rest of the Arabs. The Israelis have bombed Beirut, killing hundreds of women and children. The Jewish neoconservatives describe Israel as a bastion of democracy in the Middle East, as if the Israelis were NATO's mercenaries. No one wants to say so, but Israel now serves as a cheap army in the power politics between East and West. It is an old tactic to use native troops to defend the interests of the West in the East. Armed with Western munitions, the natives fight well, using their knowledge of the language, the culture, and the terrain.

The war goes on. The Israelis awaken every morning with their backs to the sea. The Palestinians promise to drive them into the sea, singing of holy war. The Iraqis and the Syrians and the Jordanians and the Saudis await their opportunity. The Russians sell arms, the French sell arms, the Americans sell arms. The Begin government bristles; the Israelis do not sue for peace. There is no oil in Israel; the cheapest army could become the most expensive army.

The defense of Israel figured heavily in the neoconservative argument on behalf of Ronald Reagan's candidacy. Some neoconservatives, having difficulty in moving so far to the right, used the excuse that Mr. Reagan was not only in favor of the security of Israel but would build a strong American military to oppose the Soviet Union, putting America in a position to defend Soviet Jews as well. Not long after his election, Mr. Reagan announced plans to sell five AWACS planes to Saudi Arabia. Jews argued that the AWACS planes in the hands of the Arabs would make it almost impossible for Israel to control the air in a future war begun by either side. Indeed, they argued, without Israeli dominance in the air, the Arabs would be more likely to undertake another adventurous war.

Norman Podhoretz responded to the AWACS sale in the Washington *Post*, calling it appeasement, saying the decision "is puzzling and disheartening to many of us who have looked to the Reagan administration for a new approach to the greatest of all dangers facing the United States: the danger that the oil fields of the Persian Gulf might fall under Soviet control." Max Lerner called it "a betrayal of trust."

Israel cannot remain at war forever. The country is too small and her enemies are too many. A trade of Israeli lives for Arab oil is not unthinkable—John Connally thought it and said it. In truth, Israel has no choice but peace; it is her only defense. Until peace comes to the Middle East, the tiny country of the Jews must find a way to survive. And Israel cannot survive alone. The Jews of the Middle East live at the mercy of other nations, primarily America; yet the neoconservative Jews, self-proclaimed defenders of Israel, urged that the fate of millions of Jews be given into the hands of men who call mercy inefficient.

No single event could have led so many Jews into a confusion of ethics, nor could any one event have led Jews into a narrow, parochial definition of Jewish interests, a definition that has now been revealed as potentially dangerous to Israeli Jews, if not to all Jews.

The murder of the Jews of Europe exposed the world to incomprehensible darkness. And suddenly, out of the darkness, in bloody victory, the State of Israel was born. A cold war. American Jews achieve middle-class and upper-middle-class standing. The question is asked: Are Jews still a humble people, poor, and few in number? Some Jews are tired of poverty and humility. Israel shows that Jews can fight. In a glorious moment Jews feel the relief of not having to depend on the mercy of others. All of this happens in comfort. Irving Kristol looks to Calvin for proof that Jews are rich because God wanted them to be rich. The Calvinist view of interests persuades some Jews. The fear of a small people is united with the fears of the Haves, for Jews have both a homeland in Israel and all the comforts of home in America. A group of Jews mistake themselves for the fat old men of history, sitting in their clubs, satisfied that providence has put them in their proper place, willing to condone war or misery to hold on to what they have; they call themselves new conservatives. If the world intruded upon their comforts, if they were not members of what they have called "the new class," they might not sit so easily, for it would occur to them that they may have sold their ethics for less than nothing.

In the August 1980 issue of *Commentary* Ruth R. Wisse paraphrased Y. L. Peretz's fable about Yankele and the rabbi of Chelm. She wrote:

> Once the good-hearted rabbi of Chelm was interrupted in his devotions by the sudden appearance of one of his townspeople, Yankele, bleeding and howling in pain. The shabbes-goy had gratuitously punched Yankele in the mouth. The rabbi asked solicitously if he could inspect the damage. But when Yankele opened his mouth, the rabbi was horrified. How does a Jew come to have such a healthy set of teeth? Are these the very teeth that Yankele had exposed to the shabbes-goy? Well, then, no wonder he had been brutalized. For a Jew to show such strong teeth is in itself a provocation. The rabbi counseled Yankele never to show his teeth to any Gentile again.
>
> In subsequent weeks, although Yankele keeps his mouth dutifully shut, the shabbes-goy beats him up repeatedly. Each time the rabbi, after due analysis of the situation, discovers a provocation: once Yankele had carried a loaf of

bread home from the marketplace, obviously attracting the shabbes-goy's envy; a second time he had strayed too far out of town, obviously transgressing what the shabbes-goy considered to be the Jew's legitimate bounds. Finally, after still another beating, the rabbi realizes the gravity of the situation and calls a public meeting of the local Jewish elders to resolve the matter. The meeting unanimously concludes that Yankele is too dangerous to keep in town. At the rabbi's suggestion he is forced to leave, and the shabbes-goy's wages are modestly raised to placate him and "move him to pity."

After an attack on those American Jews who oppose Israeli settlements on the West Bank, an attack that extends to any Jew outside Israel who disagrees with any action of the Begin government, she concludes:

Peretz's little satire about Yankele and the shabbes-goy was directed against the Jewish socialists and other idealists of his day who tried to justify the pogroms against the Jews by eliminating the Jewish "provocations," and to find the causes of anti-Semitism in the Jew so that they would not have to come to his defense. Israel has rescued Jews from the political condition of statelessness, but apparently not from its psychological handicaps. As Peretz wrote, there's a little of the rabbi of Chelm in each of us.

The gentlest description of the neoconservative attack on Jacobo Timerman would be to describe Irving Kristol, Norman Podhoretz, David Sidorsky, and the rest of the movement as rabbis from Chelm. They followed the pattern of the Peretz story quoted by Ruth Wisse: Timerman, a Jew, was arrested by the neofascist Argentine government and held for twenty-nine months, during which time he was tortured by men who shouted, "Jew! Clipped-prick!" as they administered electric shocks to his naked body. He was in-

terrogated by officials of the government and was accused
of belonging to the Zionist conspiracy. By his account,
Timerman, the editor of the liberal daily *La Opinion,* was
tortured because he was a Jew.

Through pressure from the U. S. Government Timerman's
release was obtained and he was deported to Israel. There
he wrote a book entitled *Prisoner Without a Name, Cell
Without a Number.* Soon after the publication of the book,
which was excerpted in *The New Yorker,* an apparently orchestrated attack on Timerman's character was launched,
along with a similarly orchestrated effort to portray the
leaders of the Argentine government as something close to
philo-Semites. Irving Kristol opened the attack by claiming
that Timerman had been arrested because of his connection
to David Graiver, an Argentine wheeler-dealer with alleged
connections to the radical left Montoneros. Graiver died in a
plane crash a year before Timerman's arrest. No charge
against Timerman involving Graiver was made by Timerman's Argentine jailors.

The real job of hit man was given to Mark Falcoff, of the
University of Oregon, a boy with half a book about Argentina before Perón under his belt, a bizarre misunderstanding
of totalitarianism to support his theories, and an as-
tonishingly hard-line rightist view of the world. Mr. Podhoretz gave him the cover of the July 1981 issue of *Commentary* in return for doing the job.

Mr. Falcoff did his work as well as he was able. He accused Timerman of publishing a Peronist newspaper and of
connections with the radical left. He dwelled at length on
the Graiver incident. He attacked the New York *Times* for
showing sympathy to Timerman. Along the way he made
the obligatory defense of the Jeane Kirkpatrick theory of
political philosophy as opportunism, arguing that there is a
difference between authoritarian and totalitarian regimes, a

difference that does exist but is not determined by the degree of hostility the regime shows toward the United States.

A tenet of the argument that Argentina is not a totalitarian state is that it bears no relation at all to the Nazi regime in Germany. Neoconservatives argue that Argentina permits emigration and freedom of religion, as if the Nazis did not permit both emigration and freedom of religion until quite late in the regime. Totalitarianism, as the neoconservative Jews conveniently forget, is not a form of government but a process. The inability of the totalitarian organization or state ever to achieve its impossible goal is one of the vital parts of the definition of totalitarianism. Organizations aimed at totality must be examined according to the processes they institute, not by the degree of control they have achieved. Otherwise the patient must die before the illness can be diagnosed. A totalitarian regime could seem acceptable to some and admirable to others in its early stages if totalitarianism is defined by the achievement of its goal rather than by the institution of methods aimed at reaching the goal.

Mr. Falcoff bases his admiration of the Argentine military on an old German argument: The communists drove them to it, and even if they have gone beyond the bounds of law and justice, they must be permitted to do so in defending law and justice against the radical left. It has been a long time since ideas such as the following have been printed in an American magazine:

> After the coup which deposed Isabel Perón the military initiated a sweep of known or suspected elements of the violent Left. As is necessarily the case in any urban setting where the forces of order must contend with the virtual invisibility of the enemy, a blanket repression is often the only means which offers any hope of success. In such situations—

let us not mince words—the distinction between terrorist
and suspect, between sympathizer and activist, indeed, between innocent and guilty, is often lost—but in the end the
job can be done, if the will is there to do it.

This is precisely what the Montoneros and the ERP never
expected, forgetting (if they ever knew) that army officers
are not vacillating liberals, and that with every kidnapping,
murder, and bombing, the guerrillas themselves were unty-
ing the last cords of professional military restraint.

Jacobo Timerman is not an angel. He is a middle-aged
Jewish man who edited a newspaper in a country run by an
anti-Semitic military government that had lost its sense of
law and limits. He was imprisoned without due process. He
was tortured. He was made to suffer vicious anti-Semitic in-
sults while he was being tortured. If his life prior to his
imprisonment was not without blemish, is that reason for
Jews to defend his torturers against him?

In the desire of the Jewish neoconservatives to please the
Reagan administration, they have printed Mark Falcoff's
approbation of the lawless tactics of fascism in a magazine
subsidized by the American Jewish Committee.

The rabbi of Chelm was a fool. If the Jewish neoconservatives were merely fools, one could be amused by them
and go on to more serious things; but these new Jews have
caught the fancy of those who are now in power in
America. They provide rationalizations to an administration
that does not base its actions on justice or mercy but on interests. The Jewish neoconservatives claim they are acting
in defense of the Jews of the Soviet Union and of Israel,
people whose only hope is in justice and mercy, for small
nations and small minorities within nations have no other
shield. If a small and humble people are eclipsed as an interest by some larger interest, what will happen to them?

Jacobo Timerman, like the basketball player of Lublin, is
an irritating man, full of demands, a cause of discomfort, a

contrary man. Perhaps that is what comes of being tortured or of eating cockroaches? To attack a man who has suffered is not the way of the people who learned shame at the foot of Sinai; it is the act of fearful and merciless people, of those who have not been able to escape the touch of darkness.

6. A Desert Is a Town Without a Minyan

My father took us directly to the garden behind the house. Look, he said, an olive tree like the trees in Israel. You know the story of the Maccabees and how the oil from a tree like this burned for eight days?

It did not make the house acceptable. Pomegranates rotted on the ground. Where the grass grew it was a foot high. Where the desert sun had killed the grass the ground was pale brown and stony. A ramshackle fence that had once been painted red separated the garden from the house next door. There were unidentified barnyard odors in the air.

The house itself was small, made of adobe brick covered with white stucco. Desert trees—two old and half-naked willows and two stubby palms—grew in the front yard. The heat outside was palpable, exactly like the heat that pours out of a hot oven when the door is opened. Inside the house it was cool, almost clammy. We were a long way from

Chicago and even farther from the plush carpeting and hot Parker House rolls of the Golden State Limited.

A mouse appeared in the living room during our first evening in the high desert along the Mexican border. My mother screamed and climbed up on a table. My sister, who was three years old, laughed gleefully, shaking her long, fat curls. My father and I chased the mouse.

In the very early morning my mother screamed again. An enormous beast had put its head up close to the screen of the bedroom window and mooed its welcome. Never had such a beast intruded upon the calm of a fourth-floor apartment in Chicago. The beast belonged to the people next door, a family of Mormons of prodigious fecundity: I never quite got an accurate count of the children; it was somewhere between nine and twelve.

The children next door were hospitable. They quickly introduced my sister and me to the local sports: catching lizards; climbing desert willows; watching big red ants crawl in and out of the cheesecloth belly of a dead horned toad; and throwing pomegranates—a deadly activity, for a direct hit with a ripe pomegranate on a pale article of clothing left a stain that no soap or bleach could remove.

There were four Jewish families in the town, one of whom owned the gloomy, cavernous furniture store where my father worked. Another family was a youngish couple without children. They lived in what seemed to me an elegant house, with sliding glass doors that opened onto a patio. He was a small man with thinning hair and a mustache; she wore scanty, suggestive clothes on Sunday afternoons. We saw them infrequently because they were rich and we were not. The third family kept to itself. We were the fourth.

On the High Holy Days the Jews of the little border town went to Phoenix or Tucson to the synagogue. We did not. We had no car, no place to stay, and no money for such a

trip. On the eve of Rosh Ha-Shanah my mother cooked a
roast chicken dinner and we all dressed in our best clothes.
When the meal was over and the dishes were washed, my
mother took off her apron and came into the living room.
My father had put on his suitcoat and his hat. I, too, wore a
suit. My mother wore a hat and a going-out dress.

My father was the rabbi and the cantor and the president
of the congregation. My mother, my sister, and I were the
congregation of Israel in that small town on Erev Rosh Ha-
Shanah. My father and I said the prayers in Hebrew. He
read slowly so that I could follow, repeating his words more
than reading. Then my mother, my father, and I said our
prayers in English. My sister sat solemnly on an old plush
chair with her feet sticking straight out and her hands
folded in her lap.

When the service was over, we all cried. I think it was on
that night that my parents decided to leave the little town
on the Mexican border for a bigger town, one with lights
and tall buildings and a minyan.

To a Zionist the homeland of the Jew cannot be anywhere
but Israel. To one who believes there is a place for Jews in
the Diaspora, the promised land cannot be anywhere but
America.

Like other immigrants, Jews came to America hoping for
religious freedom and economic opportunity. They were ad-
venturers or misfits; they were the landless and the tillers of
ungiving land; they were the people who lived on air, looking for some place to settle, to practice simple trades, or to
open little shops or just to work—anywhere for anyone at
anything that would pay a living wage. They were twice
hopeful, for they brought their children with them. In none
of this were they different from the Irish or the Poles or the
Italians or the Germans or the Czechs or the Russians or the
Greeks or the Swedes or even the English who landed at

Plymouth. They were immigrants in a nation of immigrants. Never in the history of the Diaspora had they had so much in common with their countrymen. Polish Catholics became Americans, Lithuanian Jews became Americans.

The history of the Jews in America is too well known to bear repeating: A Jew sailed with Columbus; Jews went to New Amsterdam and to Newport, where the eighteenth-century synagogue still stands. First the Sephardim and then the Ashkenazim. By the end of the nineteenth century, when the great wave of immigration began, the Ashkenazim dominated. The *Ostjuden* did not please the Ashkenazim in America, as they did not please them in Germany.

Jewish peddlers went out West in the nineteenth century and Jewish factory owners exploited Jewish labor in sweat-shops in the East in the beginning of the twentieth century. Jews fought in America's wars, from the Revolutionary War to Vietnam. There were Jewish philanthropists and Jewish gangsters, rabbis, cantors, financiers, prostitutes, jazz musicians and classical musicians, painters, poets, teachers, scientists, doctors, and patients.

America suited Jews and Jews suited America. Roger Williams, George Washington, and every major figure in American history after them spoke in favor of religious tolerance. Jews suffered from anti-Semitism in America: Some businesses, many clubs and neighborhoods, and some universities either excluded Jews or limited their number, but there were no pogroms, no expulsions. Jews were elected to public office, Jews were appointed to the U. S. Supreme Court. In the freedom of America the Jews bloomed.

Democracy fit the Jews because the Jews had for thousands of years seen themselves as equals before God. Freedom of religion fit the Jews because the rabbis had told the nation for tens of centuries to respect the worship of other visions of God. The harsh optimism of American politics fit the Jews because the criticism of this time in hope of making a better time tomorrow or next year could be traced back to the Hebrew prophets and the dream of bringing the Messiah by creating a messianic period to welcome him.

As America abandoned the cruel notions of eighteenth-century liberalism and sought new meanings for equality and justice, the Jewish socialists who came to America in the great wave of immigration were in the vanguard. The Jews brought a notion of mercy with them to America, a notion they had been nourishing since Deuteronomy and Isaiah, a notion of social welfare that they had practiced within the Jewish community for thousands of years. Now that they were a part of a larger community, truly a part of the community, with voting rights, freedom of movement and occupation, and the ability to hold public office, they extended the notion of mercy, of charity as law, to the larger community. Along with millions of other Americans Jews spoke out for social justice.

Before Jews had solved all of their own problems they worked to help blacks rise up out of poverty and ghetto life. Before Jews had lifted themselves securely out of the grinding necessities of poverty, they worked to help others gain freedom from necessity. It would be arrogant to attribute the history of social justice in America to Jews, but it would be unfair to overlook the contribution of Jews, who brought with them the ethics, developed over centuries, of knowing the cruelty of necessity and the need for men to be merciful.

All of this happened while America was growing, an adolescent in Vico's cycle of birth, maturity, and decline. The adolescent had an insatiable appetite for energy, ideas, people, and progress. America grew so rapidly that it had room for everyone. It grew into the richest, most powerful nation on earth, and American Jews grew with it. Generous, experimental, accepting, roomy America rose to the top of the order of the nations of the world—more literate, more affluent, with a lower infant-mortality rate than any other nation on earth. Now America has matured. Its wealth can no longer be increased at the same rate. It is no longer assuredly the most powerful nation on earth. The American vision of infinity has been lost in the problems of the world as it is. The mature nation must consider how to apportion its limited wealth. American Jews occupy a place in America unlike any they have known in two thousand years: They are among the rich, who must decide how and when, if ever, to respond to the clamor of the poor.

Jews in America have become a minority that no longer wishes to consider itself a minority. Jewish neighborhoods remain, although they have moved from the inner city to the suburbs. Synagogues remain, although their place among Jews has gained and lost in importance over the years. New synagogues are constructed in the suburbs; old synagogues are sold to the next wave of ghetto dwellers as Jews move out of the inner city and its decaying neighborhoods. The synagogues are filled on Rosh Ha-Shanah and Yom Kippur, but not on the Sabbath. Fewer Jews keep Orthodoxy in their lives, although many still profess to be Orthodox. Reform Judaism and Conservative Judaism battle for supremacy, although the distinctions between them are constantly being blurred and redefined. After Auschwitz, after Hiroshima, religious questions are easier to ignore than to attempt to answer; many Jews who have struggled with theodicy in light of recent history have turned away from rationalism to simple faith or mysticism. Jewish revivals are announced, followed by proofs that few Jews know anything about Judaism anymore. It is doubtful that many Jews expect direct intervention by God in their daily lives, and it is equally doubtful that many Jews believe the coming of the Messiah is imminent. The minority has taken up the style of the majority, even to the point of being as religious —no more and no less—than the majority.

Jews live in places that appeal to other people of their social and economic level. Jews prefer the same universities,
clothing stores, food processors, gourmet shops, and health
food stores that are enjoyed by the rest of affluent America.
Jews jog. Some Jews drink too much, get divorced, neglect
their children. A lot of Jews do not marry Jews. The minority wants to be like the majority, but it does not want to
disappear; and the tension of a culture within a culture,
wanting both cultures, makes Jews uncomfortable; they feel
like lumps in the stewpot of American culture. Since Jews
are not alone in this feeling of being a discrete part of the
whole, it leads them to feel less distinctive than they might
feel in a more homogeneous culture.

Many Jews have given up formal religion, attending the
synagogue a few times a year, choosing Conservative over
Orthodox or Reform over Conservative Judaism for social as
well as religious reasons, not bothering very much over the
subtle difference in emphasis on history, ethics, or the Law.
Others call themselves secular Jews and do not attend synagogue services at all. Religion does not disappear easily,
however. All questions do not lend themselves to rational
answers. Even more pressing is the idea of being chosen. No
Jew in his right mind believes that God chose the Jews to
receive his unlimited beneficence in the form of security,
wealth, talent, health, strength, morality, or special forgiveness. Yet Jews still believe they were chosen. Perhaps it
is only a kind of law of primogeniture among monotheistic
or ethical religions that anchors the idea of being chosen.
Perhaps it is venerability per se, the arrogance of the old.
More likely it is the distinctiveness of Jews that continues to
make them distinctive. To be so few, always to have been so
few, and yet to have such a major role in history tends to
make people think they have some unique role on earth,
some mission. To give up being a Jew leads to feeling ordinary, less useful, less meaningful as a person. In light of

such feelings, Sartre's argument that Jews live an inauthentic existence as the objects of non-Jews must be viewed differently in America. Who could possibly feel more authentic than a person chosen by God and instructed to be as He is, to live in His image by obeying His Law? Who could feel more authentic than one who was chosen to enter into an agreement with God?

The sense of being chosen also reinforces Sartre's argument. The majority cannot have the same sense of being chosen, for it lacks distinctiveness by its very number. If the majority believes it has a special relationship to God, it is almost as if one were to say that everyone had a special relationship, which would make it not special but ordinary; in other words, "If everybody were somebody, nobody would be anybody at all." Thus the Jew needs not the anti-Semite but the non-Jewish majority to maintain his sense of being chosen, although it is true that throughout history anti-Semites have not been unwilling to aid Jews in their sense of feeling separate from the majority.

Anti-Semitism in America has been mild, for Jews are less distinctive in America than in any other country. Jews have a history in America as long as that of any other group except native Americans; they cannot be either strangers or interlopers. The religious distinction exists, of course, but religious distinction led to the founding of the colonies in North America. No political idea has a longer history in America than the commitment to religious freedom.

What anti-Semitism exists in America came from Europe as part of the nation's imported culture. It seems an anachronism, a hatred laid to rest, but it does not die. Anti-Semitism had a fierce revival in America in this century, a revival led by Gerald L. K. Smith, Father Charles Coughlin, and the American hero Henry Ford. Jerry Falwell, of Moral Majority, said Jews would not be allowed to enter heaven. The Ku Klux Klan grows in number and in strength. The

Rosenberg case surfaces regularly. A fundamentalist religious coalition has brought big business to its knees without a fight over the content of television programming, indicating that another blacklist is not out of the question. John Anderson, the third-party presidential candidate in 1980, once tried to have America declared a Christian nation. Ronald Reagan has demonstrated a lack of interest in human rights. Edwin Meese 3d, his advisor now and his legal affairs counselor when he was governor of California, has asked for new laws permitting preventive detention and the admission of illegally obtained evidence. Some Jews have started to feel uncomfortable: the two-thousand-year-old antennae twitch when the chairman of the Joint Chiefs of Staff or a Republican congressman from California makes clearly anti-Semitic public pronouncements.

The rise of anti-Semitism, the neoconservatives have often pointed out, always comes during a period of political instability. As anyone who has read Jewish history knows, that is not correct. Political instability sometimes causes anti-Semitism and sometimes does not. Anti-Semitism has also been virulent under stable, authoritarian political regimes. But if political instability can be considered a possible cause of increased anti-Semitic feeling, one must be concerned over the economic and social policies of the Reagan administration, for there have been many predictions of disaster: inflation at a 25 percent annual rate; a greater disparity between rich and poor; a serious confrontation between the Haves and the Have-Nots. These conditions do not bode well for the nation, particularly for its Jews.

Inflation at a panic-inducing rate and social unrest in America do not make a perfect comparison with Germany before the rise of Hitler. If totalitarianism comes to America, the causes are likely to be different: the training of a cadre ready to accept totalitarianism by the steady use of totalitarian tactics in large organizations, coupled with a major disaster—either a nuclear explosion credited to terrorists, a communist coup in Mexico, or some unforeseen problem, possibly having to do with the food or water supply.

Would America under duress look for a scapegoat, or is the tradition of constitutional democracy too strong? History promises a fall, but history did not promise the American Revolution of 1776 or the U. S. Constitution. There is cause for hope and cause for concern, the latter inspired by a change of direction from more to less social justice, away from the legal protections that had grown steadily for two hundred years, away from mercy to self-interest, away from hope to avarice.

No one can predict the future of Jews in a mature America because no one knows the extent to which anti-Semitism is endemic in American culture. Polling techniques have recently been substituted for thinking about the question. A Yankelovich study done for the American Jewish Committee in 1981 reported that anti-Semitism had declined since 1964, although more people surveyed thought Jews had too much power (23 percent compared to 13 percent) and those who thought Jews were more loyal to Israel than to America increased to 48 percent from 39 percent.

As an example of how language can be used to color survey results and interpretations, what if the 48 percent who thought Jews were more loyal to Israel than to America were described as those who believed Jews were potential traitors, or who thought Jews should at least consider giving up their U.S. citizenship or should be barred from public office or from voting because of their misplaced loyalty? In fact, such polls tell us nothing at all of use. We are informed by pollsters that more educated, more affluent Americans are less anti-Semitic, when it may be that more educated, more affluent Americans have learned to answer pollsters in the "correct" way instead of baring their real feelings. Nor does anyone know what to make of the effect on polls of the growing number of people who refuse to submit to the questions of pollsters.

A poll of 1,215 people does not tell us why there were three times as many acts of anti-Semitic vandalism in 1980 as in 1979, nor does it tell us why blacks have turned against Jews—if they have. In a press conference announcing the results of his poll, Mr. Yankelovich reported that Americans "have grown increasingly tolerant of a variety of life styles and beliefs." As reported by the New York *Times,* he went on to say that "this general tolerance for diversity is strongly tied to tolerance of Jews in particular." He did not report the broad attack on diversity by the neoconservative movement. A reading of the works of Midge Decter alone should have convinced him that tolerance for diversity in America has peaked. If there is any validity in his conclusion that general tolerance for diversity and tolerance for Jews are strongly linked, it would follow that Midge Decter is fomenting, however indirectly, intolerance for Jews.

It is almost impossible to understand why a Jewish woman, the mother of Jewish children, would become the queen of intolerance in America, for Mr. Yankelovich's brilliant discovery that the whole includes its parts must be known to Mrs. Decter Podhoretz. Her stated reasons are as incomprehensible as a suicide note, perhaps for similar reasons. We think we understand why some people kill themselves, but we can only observe them from a great distance; we cannot reproduce the same state of mind in a normal person.

A possible rational answer to the puzzle is that the Jewish neoconservatives, of whom Mrs. Decter Podhoretz is only first among equals in the preaching of intolerance, no longer believe that Jews are "tolerated" in America. They prefer to think of Jews as no longer distinctive, as a part of the majority, among the holders of power. By their espousal of ideas for the powerful and against the powerless, for the rich and against the poor, for self-interest and against mercy, they have sought to achieve the proximity to power of the court Jews of seventeenth- and eighteenth-century Germany and Austria and fifteenth-century Spain. If power corrupts, proximity to power surely confuses, for people who are used by the powerful as intermediaries soon think of themselves as powerful.

To have crossed the aisle from their historic place on the left side was perhaps inevitable for some American Jews. To live on the right side of the aisle, in a place without a minyan, may prove over time to be a lonely existence. The belief that there is no anti-Semitism on the right, even the far right, may be an illusion.

7. Pinochle Politics

The two old men labored and screamed and fought over the cards as if the game were life. They were the titans, the patriarchs of the families, enemies and brothers, the truest adversaries. Louie, the older brother, was an organizer for the garment worker's union. Dan, my grandfather, owned a nonunion clothing factory.

All the children gathered in the doorway to the dining room to watch the pinochle war, to giggle at the old men shouting at each other, to be frightened by the vehemence of their words and gestures, and to take sides: the grandchildren of Louie against the grandchildren of Dan. The other players in the pinochle game went unnoticed. They were bit players, extras, in-laws.

Both men were large. Louie was heavy, with a thick head of graying hair and a face of bread dough. Dan was slim, with a square chin and deep vertical creases in his cheeks; he wore eyeglasses with fashionable frames. As each man took his turn, he wrenched a card from his hand and slammed it on the table.

Here! shouted Louie, for your sweatshop!

Nah! shouted Dan, for your union goons!

Exploiter!

Socialist!

Capitalist!

Bolshevik!

For your workers who don't have what to eat!

For your unionizers who don't know from work!

For piecework!

For shop stewards!

Thief!

Thieves!

For your Christian heart!

For your Christian head!

For fair pay!

For good work!

Nah! Dan, I'm taking this game in the name of all those who suffer the filthy working conditions in your factories.

What else? You take your union dues from the mouths of children.

The dues goes for a good cause.

To Moscow you send dues. What's the matter, Louie? You didn't have enough of Russia? You don't like having a toilet in your house?

Profiteer!

Racketeer!

At the end of the game they embraced like brothers and Louie whispered, Dan, next week I'll send somebody out; you'll let him talk to your people?

You'll send a man! You'll send goons with clubs; I'll have them shot down like dogs.

Louie, the union organizer, was the better educated of the two. He read in English and Hebrew; he had gone to night school. Dan was the better dressed; he had thirty

handmade suits in his closet. They saw each other twice a
year.

My grandfather's name was Daniel Mann. His brother's
name was Louis Mansowitz.

Among Martin Buber's *Tales of the Hasidim* are these
thoughts of The Maggid of Mezritch:

> Nothing in the world can change from one reality into an-
> other, unless it first turns into nothing, that is, into the real-
> ity of the between-stage. In that stage is nothing and no one
> can grasp it, for it has reached the rung of nothingness, just
> as before creation. And then it is made into a new creature,
> from the egg to the chick. The moment when the egg is no
> more and the chick is not yet, is nothingness. And philoso-
> phy terms this the primal state which no one can grasp be-
> cause it is a force which precedes creation; it is called
> chaos. It is the same with the sprouting seed. It does not
> begin to sprout until the seed disintegrates in the earth and
> the quality of seed-dom is destroyed in order that it may at-
> tain to nothingness which is the rung before creation. And
> this rung is called wisdom, that is to say, a thought which
> cannot be made manifest. Then this thought gives rise to
> creation, as it is written: "In wisdom hast Thou made them
> all."

Mysticism? Or existentialism in its most profound form?
Or nonsense? Did Dov Baer, the preacher of eighteenth-
century Poland, inspire Buber as the maggid had been inspired by his visits to the Baal Shem Tov? Understanding of
the between-stage is a key to understanding Buber's work,
but when the moment comes for Buber to define the between he turns to example, like a storyteller rather than a
philosopher, like a man who believes that wisdom is "a
thought which cannot be made manifest."

The reader of Martin Buber's work suffers moments of serious doubt: Can it be that the philosopher simply doesn't know what he is talking about? He seems so clear, so rational when he writes of Aristotle or Kant or Hegel. He can even make Heidegger readily understandable. But what of this nothingness, this between-stage? Is it nonsense or is it but another way to tell what the Greeks meant when they said that thinking is out of this world? Nothing can be out of this world but nothingness, which Dov Baer calls wisdom. The maggid and Buber diverge here, for Buber also speaks of the between one person and another, of the between man and God.

Where is the between? "On the far side of the subjective," Buber answers, "on this side of the objective, on the narrow ridge, where *I* and *Thou* meet, there is the realm of 'between'." He wishes to go beyond individualism and collectivism to find the third alternative, to bring about genuine community. "That essence of man which is special to him," Buber says, "can be directly known only in a living relation." For him gorillas are individuals and termites live in collectives. He wants more for man: "Consider man with man, and you see human life, dynamic, twofold, the giver and the receiver, he who does and he who endures, the attacking force and the defending force, the nature which investigates and the nature which supplies information, the request begged and granted—and always both together, completing one another in mutual contribution, together showing forth man."

Is Buber an existentialist? One can, without any great stretch of the definition, fit his work into the category, but he is of greater use to man as a political philosopher. Consider Martin Buber's view of authoritarianism and totalitarianism as compared to that of Jeane Kirkpatrick. His understanding results from the search for truth rather than opportunity: "A great and full relation between man and

man can only exist between unified and responsible persons.
That is why it is much more rarely found in the totalitarian
collective than in any historically earlier form of society;
much more rarely also in the authoritarian party than in any
earlier form of free association."

The Jewish existentialist theologian displays an understanding of the real world of politics more true and more
subtle than that of the spokeswoman for the political philosophy of the new Jews of the right. He relates politics to men
rather than to nations; his concern is with human life rather
than with the exercise of power. No society that destroys dialogue serves the needs of man in his relations with man or
God. The creature he champions is political man, and he
has found political man through thinking as a Jew about the
nature of man's life in the world. Something in Jewish history, ethics, or law has led him to the identification of man
at the peak of his humanity, to being the most earthly theologian.

Martin Buber was invented in the desert after Egypt. The
Law, as it was given through Moses, requires the I and
Thou of man and man, man and God; and the giving of the
Law, as Judah Ha-Levi pointed out, was not from God to a
man but to a nation, to six hundred thousand people assembled before Sinai; the purpose of the circumstances of
the covenant had to be none other than the making of community, the changing of slaves into political men. If one
were to describe the giving of the Law in the language of
Dov Baer, it was the time between slaveness and the
humanness of political man, nothing, the rung before the
creation of political man, wisdom.

Buber describes the political nature of the relation of man
to man in his definition of I and Thou: It teaches people to
meet others and also "to hold our ground when we meet
them." Nothing should be lost in the political relation of
man to man, no man should give up his freedom to the

other; political man gains through community, he becomes
more, not less.

Marx asked when the social contract was signed. For
Jews a date and a place can be given and Moses can be
named as the first of the six hundred thousand signatories.
The distinction that must be made between the Jewish view
of the social contract as a corollary of the Covenant and the
view of Rousseau or Locke is that in the Jewish understanding of the contract nothing is given up in return for
the gains of community. The principles of equity and democracy are established in the equality of the entire nation
standing at the foot of the mountain—no distinction is made
between the strong and the weak, the gifted and the common. Buber stresses that the relationship between man and
man defined at Sinai belongs to all, not to professors or pres-
idents but to all. In contrast to the Greek view that only
wealthy men had sufficient leisure to practice politics, the
Jews established the political relation of man to man for the
entire nation. There were no exceptions, no natural aristoc-
racy, no Legislator; the freedom of political life was established for all and the rules were established in unequivocal
language.

The problems of rich and poor, neighbor and stranger
arise immediately in a nation of political men. Shall the
stranger be permitted to enter into the political relationship
with the signatories of the contract made in the desert? The
answer is given thirty-six times in the Old Testament, and it
is always and unequivocally affirmative. Similarly, the principles of redistribution of the wealth of the nation are made
clear in the law of the corners of the field, which the rabbis
interpreted as meaning that 20 percent of a person's wealth
should be given annually toward the redistributive goal.
One may infer from the interpretation of community established at Sinai—and virtually every Jewish philosopher
until now has made this inference—that social justice is both

a result of and a necessary condition for the existence of political man, for community, for ethics, for Judaism.

The quality of political man that derives from the choice of establishing the rules of community in a small and humble people is mercy, for the humble delivered from enslavement by the strong can only attribute their deliverance to the mercy and loving-kindness of God, in whose image human beings were made. In a people so conceived, no line of demarcation can be drawn between ethics and politics, for any act that violates its ethical principles makes the existence of political man—the man who does not lose his autonomy in the unifying dialogue—improbable in any respect, impossible in its full humanness.

The modern response to a nation of merciful, political men is to expect doom. Mercy and justice are now thought by many people to be powerless. The merciful are duped, the just are destroyed, and the powerless are enslaved, say the forces of neoconservatism and reaction. History argues otherwise: Men, who are all born alone, form societies, nations, and engage in trade and alliances among nations that make for a community of nations; in every case the smallest element is a single person, and no person alone has power. Justice in the form of the love of justice has inspired men to overthrow despots and tyrants in every age; no man who lives in a just and merciful society seeks to change his life for the worse. And while justice is the sine qua non of a stable society, only a perfectly just society can endure without the meliorating force of mercy.

Nachman Krochmal argued that the Jewish nation did not follow the grim pattern described by Vico because the Jews had a direct connection to the spirit of God. Perhaps. If by the spirit of God he means the commitment to justice and mercy that Judaism has understood as its most direct connection. The power of justice and mercy is the power to endure: It creates optimism in men and it endears a nation to its members so that their love for the nation continually rejuvenates it.

Were the course of nations, or of any nation, smoothly upward toward paradise on earth, it would be of little importance for a nation to endear itself to its constituents through justice and mercy; but the course of nations has never been and never will be smooth, as Vico knew. Through the yoke of the Law and the choice of slaves to receive the Law, the ethics of political men were given to Jews. By adhering to those principles, developing them, applying them to a changing situation, and by self-criticism and acceptance of the notion of equality born at Sinai, Jews have lived in an endearing nation, one that stands, so far, as the exception to Vico's theory of history.

It can be argued—and the neoconservatives now argue—that Jews have suffered because they were powerless, because they put the Law given at Sinai before the law of survival of the fittest. If Jews had been the only people in history to suffer, the argument might have merit. The record of nations, however, argues otherwise: Babylonia, Assyria, Egypt, Greece, Rome—all have fallen, with awful suffering in the fall. The Moabites, the Midians, and the Philistines are gone from the consciousness of any but archaeologists. In the annals of the suffering of nations, Jews have been spared the worst suffering, the pain of a nation dying. What people now reveres Ea of the Gilgamesh epic, or Zeus, Isis, Aten, Jupiter, or Baal? The God of Moses is revered by Jews, Christians, and Moslems, by most of the people on four continents and by large minorities on two others. The Jewish nation has overcome the exile that cannot be overcome by any nation, according to the rules of history. It has long outlasted the Roman Empire, which should have been indestructible, according to the rules of power. In the most criti-

cal measure of the health of nations—survival—Jews have no
peer.

A nation that endears itself to its constituents through
justice and mercy need not court suffering or defeat. The
Torah does not champion pacifism, defeatism, surrender,
apostasy, or weakness; nor does it champion murder, torture, imperialism, hatred, covetousness, or vengeance, which
is the province of God and not of man. The life of King
David serves as an example. God does not ask the Jews to
go like lambs to the slaughter. The line between goodness
and self-destruction is drawn in the Bible. In life we do not
receive divine intervention or inspiration, not anymore. It is
as if God had given man the full course of instruction and
now puts him to the test: How will he respond to the
threats and opportunities of his life?

In the Diaspora the way was much clearer for Jews than
it is now. Israel does not live surrounded by friends. The
question of defense and aggression has been blurred by the
reluctance of neighboring states other than Egypt to enter
into peace negotiations. The tension between East and West
has found yet another expression in the Middle East, with
both sides maneuvering for control of the oil reserves.
Religious conflict plays a significant role, Mohammed having believed that the sword was the best means for conversion. Terrorism has put the Israelis in the morally dangerous
position of having to examine every stranger to determine
whether he is a stranger or an enemy.

The situation threatens to corrupt the nation. Xenophobia
can be heard in the speeches of Menahem Begin. The state
has split into factions: religious and secular, orthodox and
modern, right and left, Oriental and European, warrior and
peacemaker, imperialist and anti-imperialist. Operating
with a one-vote majority obtained through a coalition with
several small parties, the Begin forces have maintained con-

trol through yet another election, giving the radical defenders the opportunity to pursue the policies of pre-emp-
tive strikes and occupation of what they consider strategic
territories outside the legal boundaries of the state. The ethical position of Israel's actions in many cases is now questionable. The state that was envisioned as a model for the
world, Isaiah's "light to the nations," now seems to find that
it can no longer even contemplate that role. Being but one
nation among many, behaving as any other nation might
under similar circumstances, the distinctiveness of Israel
and, by association, of all Jews fades. One must now ask
whether Israel represents all Jews and is so symbolic of Judaism that criticism of Israel should be construed as criticism of Judaism itself. If that is the case, if the aggressive,
vengeful acts of the Begin government and the unequal
treatment of the Oriental Jews in Israel are the true, and
therefore sacrosanct, actions epitomizing all Jews everywhere, can the nation still endear itself to its constituents?
Can the Jewish nation continue to overcome the fate of nations, or is the establishment of the nation-state a tragic
flaw? The hope of Judaism would appear to lie in the relative ease with which democratically elected governments
can change.

What has been lost by Israel under Begin, and by the
Jewish neoconservatives who have now bound themselves
to those policies that trouble the endearing qualities of the
nation, is the understanding of the Law as it relates to the
ethics of the paradigmatic minority. In the Law the prohibition against oppression of the stranger or sojourner by word
or deed is joined to the fact of Hebrew slavery in Egypt. So
that there can be no mistaking the connection and the importance of it, the Bible repeats it again and again, thirty-
six times in all. History and ethics come together: "When a
stranger sojourns with you in your land, you shall not do
him wrong. The stranger who sojourns with you shall be to

you as the native among you, and you shall love him as yourself; for you were strangers in the land of Egypt" (Lev. 19:33–34). The relation of the Jew to the stranger is told in Exodus (23:9): "And you know the soul of the sojourner, for you were sojourners in the land of Egypt."

Ethics are given to the Jew as a response to history. There is nothing mythical or unworldly about the basis of Judaism: Out of the historical religion comes the ethical religion. A paradigmatic minority, slaves wandering in the desert, few in number, believing in a strange, unseen God, survives the desert; settles in a narrow, nearly indefensible strip of land; practices the rite of circumcision, which makes the acceptance of male adult converts difficult; and refuses to moderate its basic laws; it suffers defeat, exile, defeat again; finally a dispersion that lasts for two thousand years; yet the minority survives, the ancient civilization does not die.

By its ethics the nation has endeared itself to its constituents, which is the reason for its wish to survive. The nation's ability to survive also depends on its ethics born of history, which have spread to other nations and spawned other religions. Both history and the Law agree that the survival of a minority depends upon the ability of the minority to adopt a system of ethics and to inculcate that system in the majority through argument and example. Isaiah's vision of Israel as "a light to the nations" is not otherworldly advice; from it one can understand that the reward for good and evil is here on earth—surely for the minority—in that the exemplary minority survives.

Only by the example of mercy were Jews able to depend upon mercy for their survival through the centuries. The example of the powerless has meaning for other nations because men learn history, they doubt the permanence of power; the tale of Ozymandias lies somewhere in the consciousness of every man. The role of the Jew in history, the reason for his having been chosen, is that Jews are few and distinct, dependent upon mercy for survival and therefore the preachers and exemplars of mercy to each other and to the stranger as well.

When Jews enjoy the illusion of power and allow the illusion to lead them into acting as anything but the paradigm of minorities, when Jews promote vengeance over peace and forgiveness and call for the pursuit of interests over the pursuit of ethics, they are neither the Jews of history nor the Jews of ethics born of history. The Jewish neoconservatives again and again ask why Jews alone, of all people in America, do not pursue the narrow social and political interests of a bourgeois ethnic group. A Jew without the answer to that question has forgotten his name.

8. Red Water

My grandfather was born in a village in Russia in the time of Jewish socialism, the beginning of the Russian Revolution, and the great pogroms. The Enlightenment came to his village like a thunderbolt, arriving only a hundred and fifty years after it was launched in Western Europe. These great events somehow changed the life of his family, inducing his father to put him in a boarding school in Moscow.

At the end of my grandfather's first year at boarding school, when he was eight years old, he found himself abandoned. Russia was in turmoil. There were demonstrations, secret meetings, arrests, repressions. The school turned the eight-year-old boy out into the street.

It was early summer. He did not remember why he began walking south and west, or perhaps he didn't want to tell me. I have not forgotten, for he told me the story of his life so often and so consistently, in detail and language, that I know much of it from memory as other children recall the words of fairy tales. Perhaps he went south because he knew that the Russian winter might kill a homeless child. Perhaps he thought he was going home or to Kiev, where there were more Jews and where he might appeal to a charity to take him in.

He walked south and west, mostly south, for nearly three years. When he was eleven years old he worked in Constantinople, saving money until he could buy passage to Europe. The ship docked in Germany, where he found work as an apprentice to an itinerant tailor. For the next few years he traveled with the tailor, driving the wagon, caring for the horses, learning to be a tailor whenever his mentor would give him the opportunity. He lived on chunks of rough bread and whatever was left in the pot after the tailor had eaten his fill. The tailor slept in the wagon. The apprentice slept in the barn with the animals. Every night, before he went to sleep, he removed his clothing and scooped out the lice. Then he lay down in the straw to dream away the hunger pains and itching.

He said the tailor had taught him well, enabling him to work for real wages in a real shop. When he was sixteen years old he had earned enough money to buy a ticket to America. Upon his arrival in New York he bought a package of cigarettes, which cost exactly as much money as he had with him. He was a handsome young man, tall and straight, with very blond hair and blue eyes. He once said that the daughter of a wealthy German-American had wanted to marry him, not knowing that he was a Jew. That was the only time he spoke of her, and he gave no details; it was the one part of his early life that he did not repeat to me at least once a year.

Having worked for a man who gave him crumbs and left-overs to eat, and a barn for a bedroom, he did not want to work for anyone else ever again. He went to Chicago and opened a clothing factory. He was the sole proprietor as

well as the sole worker. To meet his commitments he sewed
all day and most of the night. When he had more commitments than he could meet alone, even with his long hours,
he hired a woman to help him. Soon he hired another, and
then another. In a few years he had a real factory, with
rows and rows of sewing machines, cutters and finishers,
bookkeepers, even an accountant who came in every few
months to check the books. He had a lawyer and a banker.
He bought stocks. To describe his situation to me, he said
that he lived only a block away from the Franks family,
those poor souls whose son was kidnapped and murdered by
Leopold and Loeb. He was to be wiped out in the crash of
1929, suffering a stroke on the day the margin call came,
and recovering slowly, working by himself, hiring one em-
ployee, then two, three, six, twenty, and so on. He was to
become a rich man again, with factories in three towns, but
he was never again to know the glorious, seemingly limitless
success of the time before the crash.

He did not forget his father. At the height of his prosperity my grandfather managed to locate his father in Russia,
to arrange a visa for him, and to send him a ticket to
America. The old man came from a village in Russia to an
elegant apartment in Chicago. He was astonished by his
son's wealth: He had a fine car, a closet filled with made-to-
order suits, and his wife wore silks and furs. In his son's
house food and drink were available without limit. The old
man tasted strawberry soda and fell into a kind of ecstasy.
Red water, he called it. At every meal he asked for red
water. Between meals he drank red water. Nothing pleased
him more about America than red water. Amid comfort and
affluence beyond his dreams, he found a symbol of the good
life in America: red water.

Life in America went along splendidly. The old man
thought he had found paradise on earth. He had never been

so happy. His son fawned over him, giving him limitless quantities of food and red water, driving him around the city in his large and luxuriously appointed car. Nothing was too good for the old man; no wish was denied him. At the end of two weeks my grandfather sent his father back to Russia to the little village where food was scarce, winters were hard, and no one had indoor plumbing. The old man never heard from his son again. The date of his death was not known. He inspired no kaddish.

My grandfather lived most of his life that way. He hated unions, favored Republican candidates, and used nepotism as a weapon. Only the plight of refugees and blacks could reach him. Late in life he invested in a building on one of the town's commercial streets. There was a large store on the street level, and there were two floors of small apartments above the store. The people who lived in the apartments were poor. I went with him once to ask a tenant why he had not paid his rent. The tenant's wife answered my grandfather's knock. She smiled at him, sweet and fearful. Husband lost his job, she said. I'm down to one day working a week.

I winced for what I feared my grandfather would do. He was a hard man, less forgiving than any man I ever knew. To my surprise he did not demand the rent; instead he offered to help the woman and her husband find work.

Afterward, riding home in the car, I said, That was a decent thing you did.

He said, It's between you and me and the lamppost. Understand?

Jews have survived suffering, decimation, and worse. The power that kills is not the sword or the fire but the word: Only antinomy has the capacity to destroy ethics and pervert history; only Jews can bring Judaism to an end. When a Jew writes the following, as Erich Isaac did in *Commentary* in 1980, the danger to the nation is clear:

> It is past time that Jews engaged themselves in the effort to define a Jewish agenda. Unfortunately, those most deeply immersed in Jewish law and philosophy have not concerned themselves with this matter. Yet it should not be too difficult to identify in that tradition philosophical underpinnings for this agenda, e.g., "Thou shalt not respect the person of the poor, nor honor the person of the mighty: but in righteousness shalt thou judge thy neighbor." A good principle for Jews to represent should a new constitutional convention be convened.
>
> The goals of the agenda must include the strengthening of that social, political, and economic system which has given greater freedom to Jews in their dispersion, both as Jews and as men, than any other since the extinction of ancient Jewish statehood, i.e., modern capitalism. The agenda must include the cherishing and defense of social structures which allow for the broadening and flourishing of the so-called middle class. . . .

Mr. Isaac and his editor, Mr. Podhoretz, are truly *new* Jews. For the Jews of the thirty-five-hundred-year-old religion the agenda was set out in the desert of Sinai. The Talmud offers a remarkably complete exegesis of the agenda, and there is more to think about in Rashi, Rambam, and so on. What Mr. Isaac seeks is not a Jewish agenda but a new agenda for Jews.

His method is classic. The quote, which he does not identify, is from Leviticus (19:15), and it is not about economic policy, it is about jurisprudence. Nor is it about the Jewish view of social justice, for the same chapter of Leviticus gives the Jewish agenda on that subject: "And when ye reap the harvest of your land, thou shalt not wholly reap the

corners of thy field . . ." (19:9). So that Jews will not make
Mr. Isaac's error, the same rule of jurisprudence is set down
in Deuteronomy not once but twice, as Rashi notes in his
comment on Deuteronomy 24:17: "Thou shalt not pervert
the judgment of the stranger, or of the fatherless." He
writes: ". . . and with regard to the well-to-do one has already been forbidden to do so (16:19): 'Thou shalt not
wrest judgment,' (which is a general prohibition including
both poor and rich), but it (Scripture) repeats it regarding
the poor in order to make one *who wrests the judgment of
the poor* transgress two negative commands. Because it is
easier to wrest the judgment of the *defenseless* poor than
that of the rich, therefore Scripture lays down a prohibition
regarding him a second time (Siphre)." Rashi's comment
and Rabbi Ishmael, the beautiful martyr, whose work Rashi
consults, have a slightly different interpretation of the Law
regarding the conduct of a court trial than that stated in
Commentary by one of the new Jews.

Mr. Isaac says in the same article that it is not power that
corrupts, "but it is, rather, powerlessness that corrupts." His
attempt, beginning with the misuse of Scripture, is to describe a new Judaism, the neoconservative version of morality based in John Calvin and Adam Smith. What Mr. Isaac
and the other new Jews forget is that neither Calvin nor
Smith were Jews, nor were they followers of the social
teachings of Jesus as I read them or as many Christians read
them. The liberalism of the eighteenth century transported
whole to the twentieth century can lead to the belief that
powerlessness corrupts. Jewish ethics side with Lord Acton
rather than with Mr. Isaac: Prohibitions against the seeking
of power, fame, and wealth appear innumerable times in
Jewish literature. The laws of the corners of the field, of
gleaning, of the jubilee year, and so on, have the explicit
purpose of limiting wealth and redistributing it to achieve
greater equality of outcome. The Jewish view of how to

treat the poor and the eighteenth-century liberal view (even when it comes from David Ricardo, Smith's Jewish disciple) have nothing in common. Calvinism is a direct contradiction of Hebrew Scripture, which states that God loves the poor.

The economics of Judaism are ethical rather than practical, although the practicality of economics based in ethics is often pointed out. Maimonides, speaking about the jubilee and the year of release, says that the Law has two purposes: first, "that the poor of thy people may eat" (Exod. 23:11), and, second, that "the land will also increase its produce and improve when it remains fallow for some time." The Law "concerning the relation between lender and borrower" says Maimonides, "will be found, on being carefully examined, to be nothing but commands to be lenient, merciful and kind to the needy. . . ."

In speaking of the prohibitions against mistreatment of slaves, Maimonides says, "This we owe to the lowest among men, to the slave; how much more must we do our duty to the freeborn, when they seek our assistance?" He sums up his interpretation in a sentence that would find no place in the agenda of Jews who have taken up the harsh law of the invisible hand: "For it is in the nature of man to strive to gain money and to increase it; and his great desire to add to his wealth and honor is the chief source of misery for man." That is why, in Maimonides' view, the Law requires the distribution of wealth.

The invisible-hand theory, from Adam Smith to Irving Kristol and Milton Friedman, has only to do with process. Smith prohibits ethics from entering into the process. At that instant his economics depart forever from the Jewish view that came down from Sinai, was carried through the prophets, the teachings of Jesus, and all the Jewish commentaries.

The distinction between Jewish ethics, which determine

economics, and the agenda of the neoconservatives is best made by Irving Kristol in *Two Cheers for Capitalism:*

What if we are loyal members of the kind of Orthodox Jewish community that even today is to be found in sections of New York City? In such a community, where most people are engaged in business, there unquestionably is some role for an economist—but only within narrow limits. In the end, the superior purpose of such a community is obedience to sacred Law and meditation on the meaning of this Law. For the maximization of such an end, economics is of little use.

Modern, liberal, secular society is based on the revolutionary premise that there is no superior, authoritative information available about the good life or the true nature of human happiness, that this information is implicit only in individual preferences, and that therefore the individual has to be free to develop and express these preferences. What we are witnessing in Western society today are the beginnings of a counterrevolution against this conception of man and society. It is a shamefaced counterrevolution, full of bad faith and paltry sophistry, because it feels compelled to define itself as some kind of progressive extension of modernity instead of what it so clearly is, a reactionary revulsion against modernity. It is this failure of self-definition that gives rise to so much irrelevant controversy.

The debate provoked by the writings of John Kenneth Galbraith is, it seems to me, a case in point. Galbraith thinks he is an economist and, if one takes him at his word, it is easy to demonstrate that he is a bad one. But the truth is that Galbraith is not really an economist at all; he can be more accurately described as a reluctant rabbi.

9. Yasir Arafat Is a False Pretender; You, My Son, Are the True King of Israel

We tested God from a hotel room overlooking Red Square. Come on, Lord, I said, watching the summer lightning crack the sky over the Kremlin, come on. Touch the red star with lightning, shatter the walls, give us a sign.

Rain fell heavily, swamping Marx Prospect. The five glowing red stars turned with the shifting of the wind. We counted the time between the flashes of lightning and the slow-traveling thunder, gauging God's aim. The new air of the storm washed away memories of the Augean stench of the Russian poor in summer.

Destroy them, Lord, destroy them, I said into the wind,

mocking and longing for that old activist God of my forefathers.

You sound like some kind of Southern preacher, said my son.

Joshua, I muttered, not wanting him to hear, afraid that he would not know the reference. We had settled it all by then, but I did not want to recall the tears. In that room filled with creaking Victorian furniture, in that hotel sanctified by Lenin's brief residence in Room 107, at the corner of Marx Prospect and Bitter (Gorki) Street, my son had become a Jew. I do not know what he lost there.

According to a survey made in the early 1950s by a Freudian scholar, people who have been atheists from childhood are less neurotic than those who have had God and lost Him. I no longer remember who made the survey, but it seemed as good a straw as any to one who became a father when he was still a child: God died before you were born, my son; I have said an empty kaddish, draped the mirrors, sat on orange crates; you are spared this mourning of abstractions.

We had gone north and east from Paris, a dubious radical and his thirteen-year-old son, two radicals on the rive gauche, that common comedy. M. Lévi-Strauss had fixed us with one eye and chuckled smugly over the aftermath of nuclear war. Hope is not a proper exception to the vision of an orderly mind. *Merci*, Monsieur, I will take that with me to Russia, though my luggage is already too heavy. But first we will go to a café beside the entrance to the métro at San Michel to celebrate our inconsistencies with whatever they bring us when we ask for Coca-Cola.

It had rained, so we drank tea and sat under the awning. I wrote in a notebook: Lévi-Strauss's words, a description of his office in the Collège de France, reflections about his reflections on history, nothing of my awe or the good conversation I had failed to make. It had been a meager visit;

before the tea was cold I had closed the notebook, ending the visit but for the sound of his voice. He had said the word so softly, music for the cello: Doomed.

We watched the street vendor, a Gallic hustler, we thought, so typical he should have been in the Michelin guidebook. My son Tony went to buy a souvenir from him. They talked for a while, the vendor looking over at me and smiling during the transaction; such an intimate smile, I did not understand why.

When he returned to the table I asked Tony what they had talked about.

He asked me if I had been bar mitzvah. Then he asked me if I'd been to Israel. He says he's been there, and he's going back.

Discovery or revelation, there is always the same heat, the same speeding up; not guilt but nakedness: The Inquisition accuses, the Third Reich accuses, the czar accuses, expelled from England, expelled from France, banished beyond the Pale, and now to be pushed into the sea. From the window of a tenement I saw them desecrating the synagogue, until the trucks arrived and the Jewish hoodlums recruited from poolrooms leaped out swinging baseball bats, a Stern Gang in Chicago in 1941, the defense of the Vilna Shul under the streetlight. I was five years old. On the sidewalk where they fought I lagged filberts on holy days.

Discovery or revelation, the defenses always rise: fists, though not for a long time; words now. Naked, I dress myself in words. Einstein, Nobel Prizes, violinists, cloaked in the Enlightenment, and before that the people of the Book, discoverers of God, the first to choose Him if not the ones He chose.

And that other defense: How does he know? Jews are an urban people; I have lived beside a cornfield; I have lived in a town without a minyan. Yes, I studied Hebrew, but so long ago. Yes, I have heard Yiddish, but Spanish is my sec-

ond language. I know more Latin than Greek, more Greek
than Yiddish, and nothing at all of Aramaic. Furthermore, I
refuse to accept the judgment of a vendor of two-franc
models of the Eiffel Tower; how could he have known? But
he must have been sure. He would not have risked losing a
sale. Is it because there are anti-Semitic slogans written on
the walls of the métro stops? France is an old country.

When we looked up, we could see him laughing, chatter-
ing away in French. He looked at us. You made the sale, I
thought. Look away. We did not come here for this. The
next day we left Paris.

Two years before, in 1969, I had asked my son if he
wanted a bar mitzvah or a trip when he was thirteen years
old. He had said he wanted to visit Russia, and I had agreed
to it. Some day he must also visit Turkey and Spain to find
the tradition given to him by his mother. Now it was the
Russian idea that fascinated him. He called himself a
Marxist-Leninist without having read either. When he saw a
booklet of anti-Semitic cartoons published in Russian news-
papers and magazines, he said, The Russians have good car-
toonists.

We went to East Berlin to have a look at Marxism-
Leninism there, and then by train to Warsaw, Bialystok,
Vilnius, and Leningrad. The lesson of the street vendor continued. We saw the East German Army marching, goose-
stepping, slapping its boots on the pavement. Why was it
funny in those newsreels? It is a dance step, elegant mili-
tarism, perversity. Yeats was wrong; there will be no slouch-
ing on the way to Jerusalem. We laughed because we were
safe. In the melting pot anyone is an Aryan; everyone is
pure because no one is pure.

One percent of the population of Germany was Jewish
prior to Hitler's effort at genocide. Of Germany's Nobel
Prize winners, 29 percent were Jewish. Prior to the Inquisition, the king of Spain counted several Jews among his chief

Polizei! The sound of fear in the voice of a man we knew to be courageous had impressed us.

Around another corner we saw a lighted area, two cars, a truck, and several people. We walked toward them. There were two civilians and two border guards. They seemed to be arguing. Just as we arrived the civilians went into a building and the border guards climbed into the truck. A third border guard and two more civilians, one of them a woman, appeared as if by magic. They, too, were arguing. The border guard stepped away from them, which seemed to end the argument.

He was young, no more than twenty years old. In the harsh light of the streetlamp he looked pallid. He was dressed in a field uniform, though he wore a soft hat instead of a helmet. A machine gun was slung across his back, resting on his hip. We looked at each other for a moment. It was too late for civilians to be out on the street. One of the wide plazas of socialist planning spread behind him, empty and dark. There were no lights in the buildings that surrounded the asphalt plaza. He took one step back. Please, I said, where is the Hotel Unter den Linden? He did not smile as he gave directions, nor did he reply with the usual *bitte* after I thanked him.

We walked quickly in the direction to which he had pointed. It was a long time before we were out of earshot in the silent streets. When it seemed comfortable, I said to Tony, I sure hate to ask a favor from a guy with a machine gun.

I didn't see a gun, he said.

Several people came to see us off at the station, among them Stefan Heym. A charming man, still powerful then at fifty-seven, Heym the novelist is a Jew in the style of Bar Kokhba. He left Germany when Hitler came to power, returning first as an officer in the U. S. Army, then as a defector when the politics of the U.S. involvement in Korea were more than he could bear. Now Heym the communist is a nonperson in a communist country. His work is suppressed. He is frequently fined. And through it all he continues to work, the personal friend of his official enemies, defining the perimeters of his existence with his charm, the literary chess master of East Berlin.

When I asked Heym if there was still anti-Semitism in East Germany, he said, There are not enough Jews. And if the Nazis had come for him. . . . There was no need to ask the question. If he should fall over the precipice guarded by his charm and the East German secret police should come for him, Heym would somehow produce a gun or a butcher knife or the jagged end of one of his treasured bottles of Johnny Walker scotch; one Rome or another, what difference did it make?

There are no sleepers on the overnight train to Warsaw. We sat up, playing chess, talking to border guards, customs officials, and soldiers. At the Frankfurt an der Oder station the East German customs inspector stood outside our window, smiling, saying with his few words of English that he would like to visit America. And, yes, he had heard of San Francisco. He stayed there outside the window until he had nothing more to say. And after that he stayed on, adjusting his red and gray cap, swinging his lunch pail. He was young, less than thirty. He had a wife and two children. During his off hours he went to some sort of technical school. He had never been to the West. He was not a Nazi, there had never been any Nazis. We stretched out on the seats and went to sleep. My son was safe. I had not seen the machine gun either.

There were three and a half million Jews in Poland in 1939. Now there is a monument in the place where the ghetto stood. The Polish women with kerchiefs hiding their hair and heavy boots hiding their legs, the thick women

who push lawn mowers over the deep green grass around
the other monuments of Warsaw are not needed at the monument to the forty thousand Jews who died resisting the
Germans. The grass around the monument is brown and
dry; there are dead stalks in the flower beds. The base of
the monument is cracked. Polish children in short pants
play war games there, holding on to the bas-relief leg of a
defender of the Warsaw Ghetto while leaning around a
corner to pretend murder. Tony took pictures, and I stared
at the monument and wept, not for the desecration of it, or
for the forty thousand people who died during the weeks of
resistance, but for those few who escaped the ghetto only to
be murdered by members of the Polish Resistance.

I did not hide my tears from him, but I did not attempt
to tell him why I wept. The ghetto fell fourteen years before he was born. There must be a limit to what we can
mourn; we cannot make a Wailing Wall of the world. But
later, in the hotel room, I did tell him: Auschwitz, Treb-
linka, Maidanek, house-to-house fighting, starving people
against the army of the Reich. He listened, patient with me,
attending a lecture in Warsaw on the Fourth of July. All
history is the same; the lessons of the past are abstract, the
calculus of culture. I reminded him to wash before dinner.
He wrote a letter on Polish toilet paper. There was a floor
show during dinner. We ate cucumber salad, veal, and
kasha. In the café before dinner we listened to Chopin and
watched elegant whores sip vodka. Romantic Warsaw, resurrected in defiance of Hitler's promise that it would never
rise again. Resurrected—all but the Jews.

I stepped into a ditch while running for the train at the
Warsaw station and turned my ankle. It swelled immediately. Tony had to help me to board the train. We went on
to Russia, standing in line at Kuznica like refugees, walking
through customs, dragging our luggage, sweating in the sun,
surrounded by women in babushkas and boots holding

wicker baskets filled with bread and sausage. You are the descendant of refugees, I told Tony. This is what it must have been like for them. One of my grandfathers walked from Moscow to Turkey, another bought his way out of the Russian Army. One of my grandmothers and her parents may have lived near here for a while, in Bialystok. They had come out of Bessarabia, leaving Kishinev, probably after the massacre. Later, we'll pass through Vilna, where one of my grandfathers lived. He smiled at the thought of his Russian antecedents, considering Lithuania as Russia. When the train pulled in, he looked at the red star on the front of the engine. He was delighted. In a few minutes we would be inside Mother Russia; that was what he had come to see.

His excitement was spiked by the Russian border guards. The train was halted in the middle of an open field between Kuznica and Grodno. The border guards climbed out of their jeeplike vehicles and boarded the train. Two officious punks went through our section of the train, searching everything, under the beds, behind the doors, clicking their heels, demanding passports. Their uniforms were smart, their boots polished, two kids carrying rifles, snarling. The only word that passed between us was *pazhalusta* (please), but it was an order when they said it.

The health officer came next, demanding vaccination cards. For a moment Tony could not find his. He trembled, frantically going through his pockets, spilling the contents of his passport case on the bunk. Take it easy, I said. The worst that can happen is that you'll get a free vaccination. His hand was visibly trembling when he finally found the card and passed it to the health officer. There was no reassuring smile. It seemed that the man enjoyed the fright of a child.

The train moved on to Grodno. I tried to tell Tony that it was better to feel anger than fear. They're pigs, I said. But he could not be angry. He had been flung out of what he understood as a melting pot, he wanted identity, and he had chosen Russia. States are not enough; we need nations.

The customs inspectors came aboard at Grodno. Again Tony was frightened, pawing frantically through his luggage to find items that had to be declared. But this time his fright was justified. We were carrying English translations of books prohibited in the Soviet bloc countries and the manuscript in English of a speech by Stefan Heym. There could have been trouble. The customs inspector found the manuscript and passed it to another inspector who waited outside the compartment. Just then the public address system inside the train came on, loud and startling, playing the Russian national anthem. The customs inspectors, who had been sitting down while filling out their forms, leaped to their feet. Tony and I could barely restrain our laughter. In the vestibule the inspector of manuscripts turned the pages of Heym's speech, watching me rather than the pages. I realized that he could not read English.

They were unpleasant people, most unpleasant when they found a poster that Tony had bought at the Russian-German Friendship House in East Berlin. *Pazhalusta!* the chief inspector said, motioning to him to unfold the paper. It was folded four times. After each unfolding the inspector became more irritated. By the time the paper had opened to three and a half feet and still showed only the blank side, the inspector was in a rage. *Pazhalusta!* he shouted, sure that at least he had found some contraband among these suspicious books and papers. Tony let the last fold fall open, revealing a bigger-than-life portrait of Lenin. His hands were trembling, but he was laughing: Lenin had saved him from the Leninists.

The train rolled past great forests and fallow flatlands. Poland had looked like Illinois before the invention of the tractor. The Russian countryside was even less efficiently used, intractable, even wild. The train stopped at Vilnius. It was very late but still light. In Leningrad it would not get dark at all during that part of the summer. We looked out at the railroad station. An old Jew stood there, waiting, looking down the track, his hands clasping a book to his chest. He wore the wide-brimmed black hat, long beard, and side curls of the Ḥasidim. His face was stony, fierce, in search of the old wrathful God of the prophets. The sky behind him was red. The light was wan, whitening his beard. He did not look at the passengers leaving the train but kept his eyes fixed on the place where the track disappeared into the horizon, waiting. He must be mad, I thought. Did he expect the Messiah to arrive on the next train from Warsaw? The Ḥasidim are all slightly mad. Then it occurred to me—I don't know why—that he was waiting to go to Israel.

The conductor-porter brought us tea and sweet crackers before bed. Tony gave her a Kennedy half dollar and tried to tell her that he liked her, but he confused the verb with the preposition, and got only laughter for his painfully composed Russian declaration of friendship. After she left, he quickly fell into a deep sleep; it was nearly midnight, and we had awakened at five in the morning to catch the six o'clock train out of Warsaw. I lay awake a long time, watching him. My ankle was swollen, discolored, and so painful I was unable to sleep.

In the darkness, listening to the sound of the train, cursing the Poles for putting a ditch down the center of the railroad platform, I smoked Polish cigarettes and sipped cold and bitter tea. I retrieved the old Jew at the railroad station to look at him more closely. He bore a strong resemblance to my great-grandfather, the one who had fled the 1903 massacre in Kishinev. It was from him that I had inherited the urge to be a writer. He was something like a rabbi, they said when I was a child. Later there was a sort of confession: He had not exactly been a rabbi. He had been a

professional mourner, a frequenter of cemeteries who
earned his living by crying over the graves of strangers: ten
kopeks for a silent tear; a ruble for weeping; the tenth man
at every minyan he attended. Did he earn enough money
after the massacre to bring his family to America? Or had
he been put out of work by the sudden spate of amateurs?
Had he ever wept for a Russian who was not a Jew?

The old Jew fled, replaced by the faces of Russians: the
border guards, customs inspectors, and an ugly, hairless
man in the dining car. We had no common ancestors. Tony,
I said softly, careful not to wake him, you will discover one
day that you are not descended from Russians but from
Jews who happened to live in Russia. And if you do have
Russian blood, it entered the line when a Cossack fell on a
Jewish woman and raped her. It's either history or racial
memory, but I know it's true. This is not home. And where
is home? On his mother's side Tony is descended from
Sheikh Sason ben Saleḥ, who is descended from Abraham
Sason, the Venetian mystic who claimed to be a direct descendant of Shephatiah, the fifth son of King David. I
laughed aloud at the thought of traveling with royalty, and
a Marxist-Leninist king at that!

In the morning the king and I found ourselves covered
with soot, the beginning of a bad day. The guide, porter,
and car promised by Intourist did not meet us at the station,
and when we finally arrived at the hotel it took us five and a
half hours to check in. The beauty of Leningrad escaped us
immediately: At the clinic a fat Russian woman, who may
have been a doctor, wrapped an ineffectual piece of gauze
around my ankle and sent me limping off; the Hermitage
was as crowded as the New York subway, though not so
airy; Dostoyevsky was only in the process of being resurrected, so the guide was forced to take us off the usual tour
route to look for the places where he had lived and set his
novels, leading us into grim side streets, ancient and rotting

buildings with unhinged doors and dank passageways, past
old women shovelling cement, and through ad hoc markets
selling vegetables, flowers, and homemade clothing.

Two Polish students we had met on the train came to
visit us at the hotel. We had offered them a copy of Jerzy
Kosinski's *The Painted Bird,* which they had refused. Now
they wanted the book, explaining that one of the other students, a buxom girl, was an informer, and they were afraid
to take the book in her presence. We became friends. They
were bright, charming—graduate students in economics; one
of them had also published two screenplays. We walked the
streets together in the evenings. They talked of Grotowski's
concept of theater and of workers sleeping in the factories
in Poland. They told Tony how to recognize secret-police
agents. In the strange blue light of the white nights, walking where they were sure no one could overhear them, looking always to be sure they weren't being followed or spied
upon, they told Tony about socialism. When we hired a car
to drive them back to their student quarters, they asked us
not to say their names in the presence of the driver and instructed him to leave them at a place nearly a mile from
where they were staying, all to keep him from reporting
that they had been in the company of Americans. When we
were in the company of our guide at the Summer Palace at
Petrodvorets and saw them, they tried to pretend they
didn't know us, but one of them had already spoken to us
before I introduced the young lady sitting next to Tony as
our guide. After they had gone, she asked us several times
who they were. Tony said, They helped us on the train after
my father sprained his ankle. I don't know their names. He
looked to me for confirmation. I smiled; his understanding
of Marxism-Leninism was growing.

Every day our guide and our driver took us to see the
remnants of czarist Russia. The guide diligently gave us the
heights of domes to the centimeter, historical information to

the day and hour. She told us that she lived in the New Regions with her mother, who was a doctor, and that she would finish her studies in one more year, becoming a teacher of English at a salary of one hundred rubles a month. (At the Univermag on Nevsky Prospect a cheap pair of shoes cost forty-two rubles.) It was a job for her, nothing more, and it was the first time she had done it. Every morning before she met us she went to the library to memorize the details of the tour. And every night, we were sure, she went to the Intourist or Komsomol office to report what we had said. But we grew to like her anyway. She was so thin, so desperate to be fashionable, so hard pressed to laugh. She had two summer dresses, short, lank red hair, sour breath, and she wanted very much to be able to follow Faulkner's sentences. She took us to graveyards to see tombstones made of airplane propellers and pieces of machinery, and she took us to side streets to buy kvass out of great tanks presided over by sturdy old women.

On the morning of the general tour of Leningrad, between the Aurora and the Finland Station, I said to her, We would like to visit the synagogue.

Oh, it's not on the tour.

Then let's add it to our tour.

It's out of the way.

The car can go anywhere.

We have only three hours, and we should see the New Regions.

I would rather see the synagogue.

She and the driver spoke in Russian for a long time. Then nothing more was said about the synagogue. On the way back into the city from the New Regions, which are industrial parks with adjacent housing projects, the bleak highrise products of the slide rule of socialism, gray monoliths pocking a savannah, I asked again about the synagogue.

We are going there now, she said.

It is a gray building on a small street only a block from
the great Leningrad Art Theater. We stepped out of the car,
stretching over muddy puddles in the street. Our guide
went ahead to look for someone who would take us into the
building. She found three old men standing together in an
alleyway, spoke to them for a moment, then beckoned to us
to join them. Acting as translator rather than guide, she
went with us and the old men into the foyer of the synagogue. It was dark and bare, cold. There was a urinous
odor.

It was the shul of my childhood, but dead. Where were
the children? Where was the gossip? Whose bar mitzvah
was today? A little schnapps, a few cookies, please, and
light; how can we read from the Book in darkness?

Shalom, Shalom, we said to each other. Three tiny old
men in double-breasted suits and fedoras, three colorless old
men all in a row, holding out arthritic hands dappled with
spots of age.

I am the president of the synagogue, said the first man
through the interpreter.

I am the vice-president, said the second.

And I am the secretary, said the third.

In the Soviet Union Jews have the same rights as other
citizens, said the president, as if I had asked.

How old do you think I am? asked the vice-president.

Sixty-three, I guessed.

Seventy-one, he said.

And how old do you think I am? asked the secretary.

Sixty-seven.

Seventy-three, he said.

And the president was only sixty-eight. I looked at Tony;
he, too, was bewildered. Had we come eight thousand miles
to play guessing games with three dotty old gnomes? I
looked in the faces of the old men. No, they were not mad.
They stood quietly for a moment, watching me, waiting for

something to appear in my face. They smiled, wistful and indulgent. Did they want a donation? Was I expected suddenly to break into fluent Hebrew or Yiddish? Did they just want us to go away?

Are there many members of the synagogue? I asked.

Yes. There are twenty.

And how many come to prayer services?

Many, all of the members.

This is a fine synagogue, I said.

Oh, yes, much better than the synagogue in Moscow. You are going to Moscow?

Yes.

And have you been to Israel?

No. But I plan someday to visit there. Meanwhile, I'm planning to write about my grandparents, who lived in Russia. May I come back someday to talk with you about Russia in those times, around the turn of the century?

For that you should read Sholom Aleichem.

Well, perhaps I could come back again before I leave.

We won't be here, said the president. It was the end of the visit. They patted Tony on the head, they shook my hand, and they showed us out.

In the car, driving back to the hotel, Tony and I were silent. We would not go back. Every writer suffers the jackal lurking in his head, but it is the easiest of the moral sicknesses to survive; I would not compromise them for the sake of a paragraph or two. By visiting the synagogue we had let the Russians know that we were aware and concerned. What had passed between us and the three old men I did not know. Had it been a conversation of opposites and tangents, a paranoid code passed through our interpreter? It was a possible interpretation, and it was given credence by three other incidents that occurred before we left Leningrad.

Our driver, who had made it quite clear that he did not

understand English, became upset after we got into the car
the following day. He turned around to speak to Tony,
pointing at something and repeating the same sentence over
and over in Russian. Though Tony had studied Russian, he
could not make out what the driver was saying. Finally the
driver said, Please close the door. He spoke with a slight
British accent. Tony and I looked at each other, incredu-
lous; then we both looked at our guide, who turned away.

That evening, following dinner with the Polish students,
Tony and I went for a walk along Nevsky Prospect. It was
after ten o'clock, but still light, and there were people in the
street, a sight we still found encouraging after the dead,
empty streets of East Berlin. Tony spied a *voda* machine
that also dispensed lemonade, and he ran ahead to wash the
glass and get his three kopeks' worth of the overly sweet
stuff. A dark, thick man coming from the opposite direction
stopped and spoke to me in Russian. I answered that I did
not speak Russian. His eyes narrowed. He staggered one
step closer. Israeli, he said.

Nyet, American.

Over his shoulder I could see Tony, holding his lemonade, watching.

The man came nearer. There was stubble on his cheeks,
his lips were parched. He stank of belched liquor. His neck,
coming out of an open collar, was thick and deeply ringed.
Israeli, he said again, insisting, jabbing his forefinger at me.

Nyet. Was I wearing an invisible tallith? a yarmulke? My
fly was closed; anyway, almost everyone in America is cir-
cumcised.

He made his hands into fists, setting himself, squaring off,
talking loudly in Russian, angry. We were about the same
size. I had a sprained ankle and he was drunk. The sonofabitch, I thought, the sonofabitch Cossack. Let him come. I
had wasted part of my life wrestling in high school and college; now it would be vindicated. I waited for him to come,

calculating the sidestep and pivot on my left foot, planning to break his neck.

Two other Russians suddenly appeared and grabbed his arms, pulling him backward, bowing and apologizing to me as they went. I watched my would-be assailant. The fury had not left his face.

I limped over to the *voda* machine, where Tony was still standing. Fucking anti-Semitic Russians, I said, sweating, spewing away the unresolved adrenalin, feeling the giddy high of subsiding violence.

Tony looked surprised. I was watching you, he said. I didn't see anything.

The day before we left Leningrad our guide spoke to us in Yiddish. *Noch a mul?* she asked Tony after he had finished one of the small dishes of ice cream served as dessert in the hotel. Tony does not understand Yiddish, so he was unable to respond. I waited to see whether she would go on, how she would explain it. Was she about to confess that she was Jewish, or did she want to know whether we spoke enough Yiddish to have made further conversation with the three old men at the synagogue? But she only blushed and said, That's German.

Oh, is it? I'm sorry, neither Tony nor I speak German.

Nothing more was said. We walked outside, quiet after days of chatter, no more measurements or dates to be learned, no more questions to be asked. Tony took her picture. She gave us her address. I promised to send her a book by William Gass. We said good-bye.

Moscow bears a remarkable resemblance to the Bronx. The Russian taxi drivers even refuse to pick up blacks. Though the politics of Moscow are fascinating, the daily life of the city is incredibly dull. It is not inconceivable that the paranoia created by the secret police is the only thing that keeps the city from falling into catatonic apathy.

The *Literary Gazette* is staffed with charming assassins.

The English section of the Writers' Union is rude. The Tolstoy Museum is clogged with incorrigibly garrulous old ladies in babushkas. At the house where Dr. Chekhov lived, a lovely woman, more careful of her beauty than any other woman I saw in Moscow, leads visitors past the exhibits. She sighs beside his bed, her bosom heaves when she speaks of his years in Paris, and when she comes at last to the time of his illness and death tears gather in her eyes, threatening to run blackly down her powdered cheeks. It is such sweet necrophilia compared to the worship of Lenin.

We had been in Moscow for several days by Friday night. There was some tension between Tony and me. I was tired of the rudeness, intransigence, and inefficiency of the Russians, and I hated them for their anti-Semitism. Tony remained fascinated. He did not mind that foreigners were barred from entering the public library or that they took an 11 percent commission when cashing American Express Travelers Cheques. He did not mind when the waitress brought out a great platter of quartered lemons when we asked for lemonade, nor was he upset to find water dripping from the ceiling in our hotel room. He mourned with them for their losses during World War II, and when he heard that the façades of the buildings on Gorki Street were made of red granite that Hitler had ordered from Finland for the monument that would mark his conquest of Moscow, he was proud.

The dispute that had begun over the border guard's machine gun in East Berlin had been exacerbated by the incident on Nevsky Prospect. I did not understand the meaning of his responses, and he was unable to tell me. Why did he refuse to see? I tried to make a joke of it: Leninism dulls your senses; it is the opiate of the masses. He did not laugh. I tried to analyze it with him, but it was too soon. (Later I would hear his fear in other voices, and the concatenation would lead to investigation, perhaps understanding.) He intimated that I was lying because I didn't like the East Germans or the Russians. I asked him if he was fond of the East German government. We looked for another answer. There was none.

We wrote letters, listened to the radio for a while, then got ready for bed.

Let's set the alarm for seven tomorrow. I want to have breakfast before we go to the synagogue.

I don't want to go, he said.

Are you tired?

No.

Then why don't you want to go?

I'm not Jewish.

Of course you are; your parents are Jewish.

That doesn't make any difference, he said. I'm free to be whatever I want.

He sat on his bed, still dressed in his underwear, holding his pajamas in his hand. His hair was mussed, curly, out of control, as usual. The signs of adolescence were on his upper arms. Thick muscles were beginning to shape his arms and legs. Tufts of hair had recently appeared under his arms. My son, verging on manhood, bright and gentle, in many ways so strong.

We are barely a generation apart—twenty years and eight months. We are at war together against an insane world; is there no way for us not to be enemies as well as comrades? For a long time I did not answer. I am a slow-thinking man, easily surprised. I wanted him to be free as much as I want to be free myself. More. Being older, I am responsible for increasing his freedom. But I had not succeeded, not for either of us. Rousseau was whispering to me: "Man is born free, and everywhere he is in chains." No, no, not free. Even that is a dream. Here was my own son demanding a freedom he could not have merely because he was my son. He was not even free to make himself safe.

Why was he afraid? Why was I afraid? Is the fear in our genes or do we believe history? Pogroms for me. For him the Inquisition too.

We looked at each other, looked away, far from home, weary; it was not a confrontation that either of us wanted. Let him believe he is free, I thought. Let him feel safe even if it is only a dream. But that is the greatest danger, the real triumph of fear, the sickness that creates the docile victim.

Finally I could do no more than tell him what I believed to be true: I wish you were free, Tony. But you can't escape. If you don't define yourself, you'll be defined from outside. People have tried to escape it before, in Germany, in Spain. You know what happened.

But it's a religion, and I don't believe in it. So I'm not a Jew. He began to cry: rage or fear or pain; it is impossible to know precisely the source of another person's tears.

It's more than a religion! I didn't know what to say. I hid in pomposity, talking about subcultures, about nothing, trying to smother the trouble in dulling words. Later, when we had returned to America, I would think about it, discovering myself in argument, arriving at advice for my son.

I don't know the culture, he said. I don't speak Hebrew or Yiddish. I don't even know the holidays. I'm free. I'm free to be whatever I want. Tears fell from his eyes. Mucus distorted his voice. He clenched his fists, the hands too large for a child but without the knuckles of a man.

How was I to define a Jew for him? It is not a history for children.

Nothing was resolved. His tears subsided. He changed into his pajamas. We turned off the lights and he went to sleep. After a while I got up and walked over to his bed. I touched his temple. His hair, dark and curly and thick, as mine had been, as my father's had been before me, was damp, cooling him in sleep. In the morning I would go to face his fear.

There were fifty, perhaps seventy-five, people in the synagogue. Most of them were old, shabby even on the Sabbath. But there was a light over the Ark, and a rabbi with a great black-and-white beard, fierce as an Old Testament vision, sat in a high-backed chair beside the Ark, staring out at the congregation while the cantor chanted the prayers for the Sabbath.

The beadle, a sleek, quick little man in a gray suit, gave me a yarmulke and a siddur, telling me several times that I must return the prayer book. I nodded that I understood—books in Hebrew are no longer printed in the Soviet Union. We spoke only a few other words: What part of America was I from? Had I been to Israel? It was forbidden for him to go to Israel. He was in a hurry; it is the nature of beadles. With quick little steps he led me to a chair in front of the first pew, opened the siddur to the proper page, then scurried up to tell the rabbi that there was an American in the synagogue. The rabbi and I exchanged smiles.

I spoke the prayers perfunctorily, following the Hebrew text, mumbling responses in the tradition created by men for whom the words come like breath. When we stood for the silent prayer, I looked around me. They were faces I had already known: my uncle Phillip, who left his business to spend his days with the Talmud; the old men of the Vilna Shul, rocking and bowing, body and soul in supplication, the gray hats in lieu of yarmulkes, the great noses, lined cheeks, frayed collars, arthritic hands, fouled consonants, tired eyes of the faithful.

There were no cowards in the synagogue that morning. I stood with defiant men who prayed not for mercy but for justice. Egypt, Babylonia, Rome, Spain, Russia, Germany, and now Russia again; we are like the despised insect that survived the ice age unchanged; we go on while our grand enemies become history. We are few, but we are not meek, even in death. Our power is survival, life.

The cantor sang the Ninety-first Psalm. His voice cracked, straining to the ancient melody. His song soared on the power of immanence.

> *Thou shalt not be afraid of the terror by night;*
> *Nor of the arrow that flieth by day;*
> *Of the pestilence that walketh in darkness,*
> *Nor of the destruction that wasteth at noonday.*
>
> *A thousand may fall at thy side,*
> *And ten thousand at thy right hand;*
> *It shall not come nigh thee.*

Several months after we returned to America, I wrote these admonitions to the king:

Israel is a kingdom of the mind. Jerusalem is a metaphor, the promise of justice.

You are but one king among many; all Jews are equal before the ancient immutable law.

Though we are a hybrid people, we internalize history, and our history has made us afraid, limiting our freedom to be conquerors, restricting our capacity to rationalize evil. Being powerless and equal, we are the mirrors of each other, we are unable to escape guilt.

Our only political passion is justice, making us gadflies by birth, putting us in constant danger.

It is an ancient and honorable tradition, but it is a difficult way to live. We can escape into Zionism or self-hatred. We can abandon ourselves to process or delude ourselves into security by joining our enemies. We can hide in blindness. Or we can remain part of the nation without a state, the arrogant meek, the wards of justice.

Those are the choices. Kings are free.

That was ten years ago. There was no need to include admonitions about mercy then: The ethics of our fathers had not been challenged.

10. Another Sasson in Toledo

People without power make gestures: We had agreed not to go to Spain until Franco was deposed or dead. The years of the gesture put the weight of sententiousness on our trip. We were prepared to see free people dancing in the streets. We did not expect that the first sign of freedom would be soft-core pornography blooming in legality.

We came upon Madrid at dawn, pilgrims in a plane strewn with the confusion of the traveler's night. Clouds lay heavily over the north and east, formed and dark above the high plain, reddening in the romantic birth of the Spanish day. We could not see the sun. The city lay in shadow. Tears ran down my wife's cheeks. She said, I've been away for a long time.

By the romantic calendar it had been almost five hundred years.

Her first language was Spanish in an ancient form. She

has an appetite for fourteenth-century meals. Even in her American clothes, walking at her determined American pace, the Spaniards in the cafés and shops were to address her in their shared language, reading a common ancestry in the color of her eyes, the thrust of her jaw, and the layers of secrets revealed but not told in her laughter, which was like their laughter.

In the Hotel Ritz they did not know what to make of this American woman whose mouth had the potential of their mouths, this stranger who could sing their songs if she liked. Perhaps they said to each other that she had been away for a long time, like someone whose ancestors had traveled with Cortés. Watching their faces when she spoke to them, I saw the masks that separate Spain from Europe.

From the quiet, tended beauty of the great boulevard, stately as an ancient general, we walked into the old streets of Madrid, up the hills and the steps and through the arches to the Plaza Mayor, there to sit in the first warm sun of spring, to be surrounded by shops of hats and restaurants serving baby lamb and tiny Spanish potatoes. Five hundred years before we took our ease in the Plaza Mayor the fires of the Inquisition had burned there. Now groups of young men in sixteenth-century costume played guitars and sang the songs of old Spain in sweet unison to remind the Spaniards in the plaza of their past—of the music, not the fire.

We put off going to Toledo several times, as if we expected something to happen there, although we told each other it was because we expected nothing to happen there.

Some historians say the first Jews arrived in Spain two thousand years ago. Others put the arrival of the Jews back by five hundred, seven hundred, or eight hundred years to the first trading expeditions on the Mediterranean. There were Jews on the shore near Barcelona when the Romans

arrived. Whoever came to conquer Spain was greeted by
Jews. Only the Jews did not attempt to conquer; only the
Jews did not attempt to impose their religion on strangers.
It is impossible to know why. They were not always the
few, not if they arrived as early as historians say. Perhaps
they always thought of themselves as sojourners. We cannot
know. There is no chronicle of the beginning of the Jews in
Spain.

It is said that the Jews chose to settle in Toledo because
the geography of the place reminded them of Jerusalem.
Some say the name of the city derives from the Hebrew
word for history. There are others who say the Jews chose
Toledo because the land is a natural fortress, a great rock
surrounded by a river, rising suddenly out of the green
plain. *Post hoc, ergo propter hoc,* the logic of history.

From some vantage points on the heights near the Plaza
de Zocodover, perhaps looking through an arch or a narrow
window, Toledo still belongs to the Jews who built the city
of narrow stone streets and gray buildings shutting out the
sun. The centuries are marked in the streets: the looming
stone, then brick, then the whitewashed façades of Moorish
Spain, and then the river, the orchards, and the green fields
that the river feeds. It is still the city that El Greco painted,
under the same clouds, under the same sun. It is still the
city that once held two Jewish quarters, where Isabella's
jewels were taken in pawn, where Judah Ha-Levi wrote the
first poems in the Spanish language; and it is the city of the
Rachels, she who enchanted a Spanish king and she who
went mad when her father killed her Christian lover and
whose weeping may still be heard in the Street of the Bitter
Well; and it is the city of Jews made to live within a walled
quarter and Jews slaughtered by the hundred and Jews
defending the gates until their attackers abandoned the
siege.

It is a long walk down through the narrow streets from the Plaza de Zocodover to the Sinagoga del Transito. The synagogue sits on low ground, open to the sun. The façade is of brick and the entrance is small and unimpressive. It is a museum now. Beyond the great rectangular room where the Ark was placed, where the walls are decorated in the Mudejar style, where the women sat unseen in balconies, is a long, narrow room of glass display cases.

My wife did not want to enter the synagogue. I do not know why. I do not know what she heard or saw or sensed in that ancient building. She said very little all that day. At times she seemed a stranger.

We had come so far; it seemed foolish not to look inside. She went reluctantly, glancing around her, as if she expected to see someone she knew or perhaps to encounter some ancient disaster. Her eyes were darkened with premonitions.

The glass cases of the tiny museum held stones in which Hebrew letters had been cut by unremembered stone carvers, wedding dresses of women six hundred years dead, silver breastplates of torahs long since burned or faded into dust. At the far end of the museum room was a history of the Jews of Toledo in the form of a list of those who had distinguished themselves in art or commerce. There had once been ten synagogues in Toledo; only two were still standing, and one of them was now a church: All the Jews of all the centuries of Toledo were now members of the congregation of the museum.

We looked through the names. Sylvia, my wife, commented on how familiar they were: Ha-Levi, Pereira, Hasdai, Caro. The names were arranged according to the centuries in which the prominent men of the community had lived. She found him, the one with her name, in the fourteenth century: Ibn Sason, 1350, poet.

Suddenly, urgently, she wanted to leave the museum. We went quickly out into the light, across a long open space to a café, wanting a place where we could speak to each other, a place to think. We could not reach each other across the years. After a while we tried to find a taxi or a bus to take us back up the hill to the main plaza. The road was hot and empty: trees on the river side, dust on the other.

We knew the direction: The Plaza de Zocodover was at the top of the hill. From the synagogue we took the street past El Greco's house up the hill toward the first of the plazas on the way to Zocodover. We walked separately. Sylvia wandered into the center of the road. I pulled her out of the way of an oncoming car. It was only the end of March, but the sun was uncomfortably hot. We came to a great plaza before a church and rested there. The hill leading into the thick of the city was before us.

As the streets narrowed and the view of the heights was obscured by the nearness of the stone buildings, we lost our way. A young girl, perhaps twelve years old, approached us from the curve of the street. Her dress was not Spanish, not of that place nor of that time. Perhaps she was Moroccan, an Arab, a visitor from some distant place lost in the ancient streets. Yet she was only a child; she could only have been of that place.

We stopped to look at each other. The girl's eyes were the color of Sylvia's eyes; they gentled downward slightly at the corners. Her skin was darker than Sylvia's, perhaps from the sun. I watched them as they spoke, seeming to ask directions of each other, the American woman and the girl in the strange, somehow ancient, dress. On a gold chain at the girl's throat, partially obscured by the white lace of her blouse, was the Star of David.

We are an old people, older than the streets of Toledo, older than the streets of Jerusalem, as old as the stones. We are an

antiquity; the reflections of us are everywhere. We can go to
the preservations of antiquity and see ourselves and know
that the makers of antiquities could, in turn, have seen
themselves in the antiquity of antiquities. Is it any wonder
that Qoheleth said, "Whatsoever God doeth, it shall be forever; nothing can be put to it, nor anything taken away
from it."

The theory of relativity was discovered by a primitive man.

Scholars make us dead. They speak of the ancient Hebrews,
a civilization long gone from this earth. Nothing is left of
the Jews but relics: history and ethics, the scrolls of a late
and aberrant sect, and a piece of a wall of an old temple.
We are dead in the way that ancient Greece is dead; and
they say we never learned philosophy.

The Hebrews were the poorest of sculptors. Prohibited
from making the image of an image of God, they did not
hew stone or decorate pottery in the way that other dead
civilizations did; disputation, prophecy, and poetry were the
arts of the Hebrews. They were the best of editors: Nothing
common survived.

The yoke of the Law was a shackle on reason, the
scholars say. The Jews did not become philosophers. God or
reason was the choice, and the choice was made at Sinai.
The Hebrews must be unearthed to be studied. If they have
gone to heaven instead of to dust, the ancient ones will be
the most surprised, for you can search the words that came
down from Sinai with all your heart and all your might and
you will not find one word about heaven.

Dead, dust, the last words so old we have lost the certainty of their meaning. The name of God was not to be
pronounced except on the most awesome occasion, and now
there is no one left alive who could pronounce it if the occa-

sion arose. Perhaps someone could have said His name at Auschwitz, perhaps He did not hear His name and that is why He did not answer.

They lied to me when I was a child, instructing me to say Adoshem instead of Adonai unless I was praying, as if Adonai were His name. Blessed be He. Who? For more than three thousand years we have been praying to a pronoun, and the scholars advise us that the Hebrews were unable to understand abstraction compared to the Greeks, whose gods were as concrete as lameness or bad temper.

I am a ghost and the father of ghosts; it is always a surprise to see my face in a mirror or to find my children susceptible to the common cold. To be a ghost with a toothache is especially disconcerting. And when I die it will be the greatest surprise of all.

A scholar as thoughtful as William Barrett says that the Hebrews had no concept of immortality because they simply hadn't thought of it. I know of no place in the Pentateuch in which the age of God is given, nor is His birth or death described. The concept of existence prior to the existence of either the heavens or the earth, or even of light, suggests something very close to the concept of immortality. What the Hebrews did not believe was that man was or could be immortal; the idea of heaven as a reward for good behavior on earth was not acceptable to Jews then or now. The good life, in the Jewish view, should endear itself to man on its own merits. When one understands that notion of seeking the good, the bridge between Greek and Hebrew thought has been opened, and one can have a different look at the later religions, with their carrot-and-stick theology and their less optimistic view of man's willingness to seek the good for its own sake.

The better distinction between Jews and other peoples might be the one that William Barrett hints at in *Irrational*

Man: Jews are a primitive people. The idea raises some immediate objections. Jews have no mythology. Primitive peoples are ahistorical and Judaism is the historical religion. Jews accepted the Covenant in writing and primitive peoples are generally preliterate. To consider Jews as primitives raises the question of Einstein as a primitive. Furthermore, it plays into the hand of the anti-Semite, who claims, after careful study, that the Jew has no place in the modern world. To the assimilationist the concept of the Jew as primitive makes a ghost of him, ending his hope for a life in the world.

The anti-Semite, loathsome, miserable beast that he may be in his goals, has the keen eye of an assassin: The Jew has no place in modern society, for he is not an entirely modern man; some part of him, the defining characteristics, belongs to that time Rousseau called "the youth of the world."

To call the Jew a primitive requires that one look at Jews through the eyes of the anthropologist, thinking of societies as circles or as straight lines without end, as clocks or steam engines, as having answers or having questions. By these measures the Jew will appear as a hybrid—ancient man the technologist. But a hybrid may not be possible except in a broken culture, in a doomed man. Once the circle is broken, the primitive man becomes something else; he adapts or dies, unless a primitive culture unlike all others exists, one that can wear the mantle of technological society without losing the humanism of primitive man. Since Judaism developed in the same part of the world that witnessed the birth of writing, the tool that broke the circle, the distinctions between Judaism and other societies of the Near East had to have come to bear on the different courses at about the same time; and the two great events of that period—the invention of writing and the adoption of ethical monotheism—

must have been the critical elements, if not the only elements, that sent the Jews on their different course.

How did Abraham become a monotheist? Did he challenge the idols in his father's idol shop—as the Midrashic story is edited for small children—and find the idols wanting? The tale seems more an adumbration of the problems of theodicy for a people who did not believe in an afterlife than a true story of the discovery of monotheism. Was Abraham a monotheist? Were the Jews monotheists during their period of slavery in Egypt? If they were, why did they turn to idolatry in the desert? Was Moses a Jew or an Egyptian? Did he borrow the idea of YHWH from the Midianites, as Freud claims?

The adoption of monotheism by a tribe of wandering traders or sheepherders in the Near East is a mystery. The second adoption of monotheism, or the reaffirmation of it by a large group of escaped slaves somewhere in the desert, is equally mysterious. Freud, in his attempt to understand the event rationally, slipped into flights of fancy. Indeed, no sequence of events, no economic situation, no sudden discovery, no catastrophe, nothing that we can divine from history or archaeology points the way to monotheism. Even more curious, only one small tribe among all the tens of thousands of tribes on earth came to the conclusion that there was but one God, that His name was not common, and that He demanded that his followers observe certain rules of conduct regarding Him and each other. The discovery of YHWH cannot be compared to arriving at the idea of an unmoved mover: One is the answer to a logical puzzle, the other a leap to an entirely new vision of man and his maker. Perhaps monotheism as a discovery should be left in the realm of the miraculous, at least until a more rational explanation can be found.

A rational explanation for the invention of writing is

available: When men had more property, in the form of
land, slaves, sheep, and other goods, than they could remember, they had to invent some form of notation. Writing
was a direct result of the accumulation of wealth in the fertile valley between the Tigris and the Euphrates. With the
invention of writing, however, other changes came into society: Not only property but knowledge could be accumulated; the world no longer had to remain as it was in its
youth, for writing made history possible. "A time to sow and
a time to reap" was replaced by "the time when." Never
again would all things have their season. History gave a
new thrust to man: change. Man would no longer be forever youthful; civilizations took on a linear form, walking
on four legs in the morning, two legs in the afternoon, three
legs in the evening, and then, as the sphinx implied, walking not at all in the grave of night.

If we believe the descriptions in the Bible and in the
Egyptian Sinhuè's travel diaries, Canaan was also a fertile
land, with the same opportunities for man to break the circle of neolithic life, if not the same pressures. Writing soon
spread to Canaan. Sometime before their exile in Egypt, the
Hebrews ceased to be a preliterate people, although not yet
modern. It was on their way back to the promised land,
while they wandered in the desert, that the Jews were
locked forever into the time of the circle.

Modernity requires more than writing: Modern man has
a very different world view from that of his primitive ancestors and brothers: Lust for property drives him, he has a
sense of an uncertain future, the rules of everyday life are
changeable, he both measures and values time, and he is es-
tranged from the concreteness of the world and even from
the reality of his own flesh-and-blood being; the primitive
humanism that endeared men to themselves and to each
other in society is only history for modern man.

Jews were prohibited from full membership in the society of modern man when they entered into the Covenant, for they accepted an immutable set of laws containing a primitive view of the relative value of human rights and property rights. Evidence of the primitive nature of the Hebrew concept of property is most clear in a comparison of Hebrew and Mesopotamian Law. Hebrew Law was the word of God, given directly to the people. Not only did God say His Law was immutable, but He gave it to all six hundred thousand Jews (by Ha-Levi's count) at once. Moses merely transmitted the message. No Jew had the power to change the Law.

Mesopotamian Law was also said to have been divinely inspired. Perhaps Shamash was the inspiration. But Mesopotamian Law was, in fact, the law of the king. It was not the code of Shamash or Marduk but Hammurabi's code. The code of a king could be changed by a king; the rules had not been written on stone tablets by the finger of God. The code of a king, by virtue of the interests of the author, saw different needs for society than the code of a non-anthropomorphic god. The king protected his property and that of his nobles and valued followers. In the case of theft, the law of several Mesopotamian societies prescribed the death penalty, equating life with property. Hebrew Law was archaic, primitive, refusing to join its neighbors in protecting property with the death penalty. And in the case of murder, the archaic nature of Hebrew Law is demonstrated again, for death could only be punished by death, a life for a life. In the neighboring modern states murder was punishable by the forfeiture of property.

The reverence for life, including the belief that the value of life is beyond equal, is impressive, but the lenient attitude toward offenses against property in Hebrew Law is an astonishing departure from the laws of all early modern

societies. Other societies took the earthly view of property;
Hebrew Law looked upon property through the eyes of God,
whose most precious creation was man, the being made in
His image. An offense against man was therefore an offense
against God, while an offense against property was merely
an offense against man.

A modern concept of property is vital to the develop-
ment of a modern state: It permits the expansionist policies
that produce great nations; it allows lives to be lost in the
quest for new property and increased power; it encourages
slavery; it foments a hierarchical society; and it always
gives rise to the urge for conquest and exploitation. The
Hebrews—wandering in the desert, without power or property to protect, legislated by God into democracy—had no
reason to quarrel with primitive law: When men are without things, they nurture their relation to each other.

Even after the Hebrews settled in Canaan, having recon-
quered their land and established vineyards, orchards,
flocks, grain fields, and cities, they could not accept the
modern concept of power and property: The Law could not
be changed. As the fortunes of the Hebrews rose and fell
and fell again, the prophets and the poets and the wise men
had no advice for them but to return to the Law, to accept
the yoke of the primitive humanism of Sinai. The Law opposed any form of oppression; it demanded the righteousness of a fair distribution of the wealth of the people
among all—widows and orphans and even strangers.

There is a great confusion about the notion of charity in
Jewish ethics. There is no word comparable to the English
word for charity. The Hebrew word related to those acts
similar to charity as we know it is righteousness. And what
is a righteous man according to Jewish ethics? One who
obeys the Law. Charity is not a choice in a primitive society; the tribe shares the wealth. Isaiah thought a person

who pursued his own interests without limit, as Adam Smith advises, was a greedy dog.* On Yom Kippur all Jews read from Isaiah 58:6:

> *Is not this the fast that I choose:*
> *to loose the bonds of wickedness,*
> *to undo the thongs of the yoke,*
> *to let the oppressed go free,*
> *and to break every yoke?*
> *Is it not to share your bread with the hungry,*
> *and bring the homeless poor into your house;*
> *when you see the naked, to cover him,*
> *and not to hide yourself from your own flesh.*

Nor is this view limited to Isaiah. In the Aboth there are two examples of what happens to those who do not obey the law of charity: Failure to tithe results in three kinds of famine; robbery of gifts assigned to the poor brings on pestilence. The rabbis had no interest in changing the Law of the primitive Jews. Nor did the thousands of years of dispersion lead Jews into the modernism of self-interest and property. For most Jews in the Diaspora it was impossible to own land, according to the laws of the lands that alternately harbored and banished them. Jews were permitted to lend money when it was considered a sin for Christians, but few Jews accumulated any great wealth even under that system. Permanent wealth, as Maimonides advised the Jews of his time, was the ownership of land—the more permanent the property, the more permanent the wealth. Since Jews were not usually permitted to own land, real wealth was out of the question for them. They had to find some other interest in life: It was to live according to the Law, to discourse in ethics, to remain the people of the Book, the

---

* Adam Smith was apparently a selective reader, choosing the phrase "wealth of nations" from this same writer.

primitives in the modern world, the ghosts who put people before property.

Had Karl Marx really been a Jew instead of the son of converts, he might have known enough of the history of Jews to understand the primitive nature of the culture and its fundamental opposition to the bourgeois notions he ascribed to Jews. He might, in fact, have found in Jewish ethics the political relation of man to man that he thought would be realized in the paradise at the end of history. In the category of anti-Semites, Marx was one of the less keen observers: He could not even find his own humanism in the mirror.

The more perspicacious anti-Semites were right: Jews had no place in the modern world. The rabbis said it was better to give charity to a man who did not need it than to risk failing to give help to a man in need, a notion that would find no supporters among the modern men who lie awake nights entertaining paranoid fantasies about welfare cheats. It is true that Maimonides thought the best kind of charity was that which gave work to a man so he could take care of himself. It is also true that Herbert Spencer's idea of charity to improve the character of the giver would have caused the rabbis to shudder in horror, for the use of charity to serve one's own interests was deemed a sin, a violation of the Law.

It was only after the death of Jesus that charity became the act as we commonly know it in America. Once Paul of Tarsus overthrew the Law in favor of the spirit, redistribution of wealth was no longer required: A man was free to give charity to the poor or not, as the spirit moved him. The giving of charity thus became a virtue. The Jew who accepted Paul's freedom to make the law rather than only to obey or disobey the Law entered the modern world completely. The renunciation of the primitive code of the Jews

was the first step on the long road that led to eighteenth-
century capitalism.

Through the long years of dispersion, Jews maintained
the tribal sense of shared wealth: In the Jewish communities of great cities, in the ghettos, and in the villages the
sense of responsibility for one's tribal brother did not dimin-
ish; systems of welfare were set up in community after community; there was always a sense of community, of unity
without the heavy shackles of collectivism.*

* Jewish communities in the Diaspora were far from communes of
perfect equality. There were rich and poor in virtually every community. Where all were poor, some were still poorer than others.
There were, however, systems of social welfare within the communities. Redistribution of wealth through support of schools, synagogues,
hospitals, and the giving of food and shelter to the poor and homeless was almost universal, although the degree of redistribution varied
from community to community. Societies that provide interest-free
loans and free shelter continue to exist in many Jewish communities.

It has been argued that class distinctions in the Jewish communities
of Europe prior to the rise of Nazism contributed both directly and
indirectly to the ability of the Nazis to preach anti-Semitism and
eventually to murder millions of Jews. There may be some validity
in that argument, but to blame the victim for the crime committed
against him seems inordinately cruel—bizarre. Yet with every new
work on Nazi anti-Semitism the argument rises anew. In the case of
the Jews of Germany, the argument also involves the question of assimilation and its relation to class. To pursue that argument here
would be useful only if it were the thesis of this book that American
Jews are behaving like the Jews of Germany before World War II,
or that American Jews face a fate similar to the Jews of Germany.
Neither thesis is intended to be advanced here. American Jews exist
within the context of history, but there is not yet any reason to believe history will be repeated in America.

Nor is there any reason for complacency: Totalitarian tactics in
American society have been recognized by writers as diverse as
Hannah Arendt and Norman Mailer. I have observed such tactics
in wide use in American business. There is a class of thoughtful people in America who believe "it can't happen here," who imagine

Jews amassed a history, but as Sartre said, Jews had no history: The hybrid man of the Law remained the primitive; sharing, bound by immutable Law to ethical behavior that was reward in itself; living, if he lived according to the Law, in the relation of one political man to another, the relation Martin Buber said existed between I and Thou. For everything that was added, nothing changed; the circle was not broken. Jews took up the idea of an afterlife, but there is less consciousness of heaven among Jews than among any other people; the great striving remained as it had always been: to bring about the messianic period so that the Messiah might come.

The Haskalah sought to modify the circle as the Hellenism of Philo had sought to modify the circle, but neither rationalism nor idealism could change the Law. The Jews remained the people of the Book—the Law was written in stone by the finger of God; it would not be changed. Nor could the Jewish view of power be changed to that of modern man; the Law was given to the powerless, suited to the powerless, given by a God who adored justice and mercy, a God who, as Rashi tells us in his very first comment on the Bible, intended to create a world under the rule of strict justice, then realized the world could not endure that way, and gave precedence to mercy.

Mercy thus becomes the most ancient, most primitive of

---

totalitarianism is born full grown and dressed in jackboots. Surely a society must be in dire straits before the preachers of totalitarian dreams can come to power, but dire straits are not impossible for America or any other nation in an unsettled world. Nuclear war is, no doubt, more to be feared, but the fear of nuclear war is also to be feared, for it could be the trigger that brings civil society to an end in America.

The New World is no longer new. We are led by old men; we are growing tired; and "when we are tired," Nietzsche said, "we are attacked by ideas we conquered long ago."

ideas, connected to the very first words of Genesis. There is nothing modern about mercy. Social Darwinism, so beloved of the liberals of the eighteenth century, is utterly merciless. Man pursuing his own interests with no other end in mind is merciless. The lust for power of modern man has no place for mercy. None of those modern attributes conform to Jewish Law, which is the law most beneficial to the powerless, most beneficial to a pluralistic society in which all the people are in the role of minorities, expected to have a political relation to each other, to live according to the precedence of mercy so that the society can endure.

Nothing in the life of Jews in the Diaspora contravened the ethics of the ancient Hebrews. There was no power; Jews survived at the mercy of the majority. There was no property; Jews had no choice but to concentrate on the relations between man and man and man and God. When the idea of socialism in a democratic political setting was exposed to Jews, it found fertile ground in the hybrid man of the nineteenth century, for it was, in its essence, nothing more than a restatement of Jewish ethics.

Irving Howe, in his marvelous recounting of the life and thought of Jews in America during the period of migration from Eastern Europe, says that socialism among those Jews was of secular origin. His case can be proved, for the lives of Jews in the Diaspora, especially in Eastern Europe, could not be expected to lead them to any other view of political economy. But Leo Baeck, during the height of the Jewish efflorescence in Germany, argued from the ethical left, basing his arguments on Scripture and on such talmudic pronouncements as Rabbi ben Zoma's "Honor is to honor man." *The Essence of Judaism* in Baeck's mind grew out of Jewish ethics, and Jewish ethics had much to do with the origins of a small and powerless people. He said that the morality of a state or nation was revealed in the treatment of the Jews who lived within it. Hermann Cohen, the humanistic so-

cialist philosopher, wrote during the same period. Franz
Rosenzweig was his student. The socialists Gordon and
Hess were also writing then, arriving at their socialism out
of observance of worldly conditions and out of Jewish ethics. Both Howe and Baeck would appear to be correct in
their appraisal of how Jews came to stand on the left,
whether it was in their interests at that moment or not:
They lived in the world as Jews and they saw the world
through Jewish eyes, which, as Leo Baeck said, are "old
eyes."

The literature of the retention of the precedence of mercy
in Jewish thinking in America is rich in both reportage and
fiction. Only recently have Jews seemingly abandoned the
ancient way. For one to say, as Irving Kristol did with a
sneer, that John Kenneth Galbraith was not an economist
but a "reluctant rabbi" is twice apostasy; first, because it
sneers at God's Law, and, second, because it dishonors man
by sneering at his observance of the Law. Nothing in American Jewish literature prior to 1967 bears any resemblance
to the work of the new Jewish conservatives, with the exception of the cockeyed monetarism of Milton Friedman.

There have always been exceptions to the rule of mercy
among Jews: Ricardo in his time; Friedman as a modern
repetition. Jews are far from perfect, as the Hebrew prophets tell us. But the prophets started the process of self-criticism that has enabled Jews to maintain their general
commitment to the humanism of mercy for more than three
thousand years. The tradition of criticism and disputation
has driven some Jews out of the nation, but it has brought
back many of the strays. When Jews support policies that
oppress the poor and the powerless, like those of the Reagan
administration, it is the duty of other Jews to compare those
policies to the Law, to lament the loss of their brothers from
the timeless circle of Jewish ethics.

The neoconservatives have pointed out again and again

that Jews in America were the only people who consistently
voted against their interests, as if the prohibition against
taking the millstone in pledge were God's error, as if the
prohibition against oppression of the poor and the stranger
were given by a fool. They forget the talmudic notion that a
wrong against a Jew is once a sin and a wrong against a
non-Jew is twice a sin, because it not only wrongs a fellow
man but puts the Jewish nation in a bad light. All connection between the new Jews and the Jews of antiquity has
vanished; only anti-Semitism makes them Jews; they are the
people of the inauthentic existence described by Sartre.

Judaism was the first ethical religion, but it is not the only
one. Jews differ from Christians, for example, over the question of the Messiah and over the issue of spirit versus Law;
but in ethical matters, in the way men live together in free
political fashion, and in questions of mercy Mr. Kristol does
not err grievously in referring to someone of John Kenneth
Galbraith's ethical beliefs as a rabbi. Franz Rosenzweig,
who very nearly converted to Christianity, described Judaism and Christianity as the flame and the ray, the eternal
life and the eternal way. He believed the mission of Christianity was to bring the godless world to the way of God
and the mission of Judaism was to preserve the people who
have already found God. The way and the life are both
eternal, but the Christian notion of original sin separates
them. The Christian is a pagan at birth and must be
renewed or reborn to become a Christian. Christianity is a
proselytizing religion while Judaism is not, for a Jew is a
Jew at birth. Christianity suits Christians, Judaism suits
Jews; both religions seek a community of love.

Through Rosenzweig one comes to understand Buber's
remark about Jews having a better understanding of Jesus.
As one who was born a Jew, Jesus had no need to be
renewed; he was given the eternal life at birth. As a Jew, he

had the Law, he was part of the people who do not suffer moral ambiguity; the life of a Jew was suitable to him. Neither to Buber nor to Rosenzweig are Jews and Christians so different that both cannot find the community of love or establish I and Thou relationships between men and between man and God. The chief distinction for Rosenzweig is the mission of the religion and the origin of the person as pagan or Jew. If Rosenzweig is correct—and there are many who disagree with him—Jews and Christians seek the same end by different means, making it difficult for a Christian to understand the moral certainty of a Jew like Jesus, who wished only to preserve the eternal life of those created for it. Following Rosenzweig's line of reasoning, the idea of converting the Jews is absurd.

How can the ancient antipathy between Christians and Jews be possible when both are based in the Bible, both seek a community of love, and so on? Religious hatred has no rational basis, nor has it any basis in Scripture. Jesus did not overturn the prohibition against oppressing the stranger. On the contrary, he stressed the attribute of mercy over the attribute of justice in his preaching of Jewish ethics. The problem of religious intolerance is a problem of modern man. Like racial intolerance, it has to do with the will to achieve power and to increase property. It is an expansionist hatred: The linear progress of modern man is infinite; he accumulates knowledge, property, and power without end. The hybrid man, with his old eyes, living under the yoke of the Law, is not an accumulator; he wishes to live a good life within the circle. He turns to his Christian antagonist, whose modern mission is to accumulate converts from among the pagans, and says with those old eyes that the goal is the community of love.

I think of the eyes of some man named Sason in Spain almost five hundred years ago at the moment of choosing between apostasy, the fire, and exile. I think of the eyes of

Menaḥem Begin directing his air force to fire into a neighborhood of civilians in Beirut in an effort to punish the PLO. To be powerless is an invitation to virtue; to be given the illusion of power is a test of reason and virtue. We are an old people, authentic ghosts; we are born Jews, possessors of the Law that spares us the tortures of moral ambiguity; since Ecclesiastes we have known that nothing prevents us from violating the Law. Mercy is its own reward, but the completely modern man wants more. To what end?

11. If Not Mercy, Then Mercy

Cruelty and highhandedness are to be found only among idolatrous pagans. But the seed of Abraham, our father, that is, Israel, upon whom the Holy One, blessed be He, showered the blessing of the Torah, appointing unto them righteous laws and judgments, should be merciful unto all. Thus, with reference to the qualities of the Holy One, blessed be He, which we were commanded to emulate, the psalmist says: "And His tender mercies are over all His works." And all those who show mercy will have mercy shown unto them, as it is said: "And He shall pour mercy upon thee and shall have compassion upon thee and multiply thee."

MAIMONIDES, *Mishneh Torah*

If we were all righteous men, Mr. Singer, we could be waiting at the station for the arrival of the Messiah, and Big Eddie would be among us, laughing and passing out cigars. He would buy a house for the Messiah and sign it over to him for a tax deduction.

If Big Eddie hired a black woman to clean his house, would the Messiah be offended?

Rosenzweig says we are the people who don't suffer moral ambiguity. Who is he kidding? Had it not been for an epiphanic moment on Yom Kippur, he would have gone ahead with his conversion. If the Law is so clear, why don't the Ḥasidim and the Reform Jews pray together? vote together? live together?

Should I cover my head? Should there be a great pipe organ playing in the background when I sing "Yigdal"? Mr. Singer, even Moses ben Maimon, the Spaniard, had to sweat to prove the need for you to slay chickens in the ritual manner. Is it better for a Jew to sit beside the sea and seek wisdom through thinking or to pray in a great synagogue, following the ritual without taxing his mind? No man has a greater sense of individual worth than the one who comes tenth to a minyan; no man has a greater sense of community than the one who finds that men cannot pray without him and suddenly realizes, in the midst of the smiles at his arrival, that he cannot pray without them.

Why is the between ineffable?

Does God hide His face from man so that we can never know His essence, or so that we will spend a long time sitting on a rock beside the sea before we discover Him?

The neoconservatives say that Judaism is a conservative religion. Do they mean that the poor, the oppressed, and the stranger must forever suffer the inequities of man's rules? Does the world belong to Esau?

Big Eddie does what he pleases. There are knife fights outside his liquor stores; men bleed and die. He cashes wel-

fare checks for women who buy sweet wine or scotch whiskey. He believes there is an invisible hand that will make
everything all right no matter what he does in his liquor
stores or how he collects his rents or takes whiskey debts
from the pay envelopes of his employees. Eddie cannot understand why anyone worries about the Law when a
shrewd businessman can slip a few large bills into the invisible hand on a regular basis and have everything taken care
of. What's God for if not to do a little favor here and there?

Mr. Singer, you were never an easy man. Scratch Big Ed-
die's back and he'll scratch yours: He plays by the rules.
Who would be foolish enough to try to cut a deal with you?
Eddie is a student of Chelm; he can look at a guy and tell
whether he knows which side his bread is buttered on.
What about you? How much did you give to Israel in 1948?
Did you put a few quarters in the pushke? Eddie gave thou-
sands; he bought a tank.

With all due apologies, Mr. Singer, you're not an economist; an economist does not pray over chickens. Your idea
of geopolitics was to say, at the end of the seder, Next year
in Jerusalem. To put it bluntly, Mr. Singer, you were too
old. With human knowledge doubling every ten years, you
seemed like a creature out of ancient history, a ghost.

If we are the people without moral ambiguity, how can
you and Eddie both call yourselves Jews? How can Norman
Podhoretz and Irving Howe both be Jews? How can Irving
Kristol and Michael Walzer be members, from birth, of the
same ethical religion? Where do Milton Friedman and Vic-
tor Navasky agree on how to obey the Law? Midge Decter
cannot even tolerate the New York *Times*, how can she tolerate Moses Hess, Hermann Cohen, Martin Buber, Maimonides, Rashi, Hillel, Akiva, Isaiah, Moses, or the God who
chose mercy over justice so that His creation might endure?

If we are utterly unique, distinct, how is it that Aquinas
borrowed from Maimonides, who learned from the Arab

philosophers how to apply Aristotle to the Bible? Was Philo
a Greek or a Jew? Why did Hannah Arendt write her disser-
tation on Augustine? If the Law is unambiguous, why is so
much modern Jewish philosophy concerned with Kantian
ethics?

Hybrids, Mr. Singer, we are hybrids, neither here nor
there; we internalize the circle and march down the straight
line. Daniel Bell says we need cultural authority; he is a cultural conservative. But which culture? of which time? He is
a hybrid man, the circle rolling along the straight line of
modern man; the neoconservatives have thrown him out of
the movement.

Can it be that everything said so far in this book is
wrong? Can one be a Jew without mercy?

Let us assume that the neoconservatives are correct in
that the aim of Jews must be to survive and that by survival
they imply survival as Jews. Given that aim, we can listen to
the argument of Maimonides in *The Guide of the Per-
plexed*:

"The general object of the Law is twofold: the well-being
of the soul, and the well-being of the body." The Spaniard
agrees with the neoconservative aim. He wishes not only
survival, but well-being.

"The well-being of the body is established by a proper
management of the relations in which we live one to another. This we can attain in two ways: first by removing all
violence from our midst; that is to say, that we do not do
every one as he pleases, desires, and is able to do; but every
one of us does that which contributes towards the common
welfare. Secondly, by teaching every one of us such good
morals as must produce a good social state. Of these two objects, the one, the well-being of the soul, or the com-
munication of correct opinions, comes undoubtedly first in
rank, but the other, the well-being of the body, the govern-

ment of the state, and the establishment of the best possible relations among men, is anterior in nature and time."

There are two kinds of perfection for Maimonides: the first, of the body, and the second, of the soul. "It is clear," he says, "that the second and superior kind of perfection can only be attained when the first perfection has been acquired; for a person that is suffering from great hunger, thirst, heat, or cold, cannot grasp an idea even if communicated by others, much less can he arrive at it by his own reasoning."

He says it is the Law of Moses that aims to give us this twofold perfection: "It aims first at the establishment of good mutual relations among men by removing injustice and creating the noblest feelings. In this way the people in every land are enabled to stay and continue in one condition, and every one can acquire the first perfection. Secondly, it seeks to train us in faith, and to impart correct and true opinions when the intellect is sufficiently developed."

Ethics must precede metaphysics. That is what he means when he says, "Cruelty and highhandedness are to be found only among idolatrous pagans." If men are not merciful for the sake of men, they must be merciful in order to know God. Mercy is not only the Law, it is one of the immutable criteria for being a Jew. Mercy is the distinctiveness of Jews; it has always been so and it will always be so. Jews without mercy are not Jews.

Isaiah sums up the ethics, the politics, and the theology:

> Woe to those who decree iniquitous decrees,
>> and the writers who keep writing oppression,
> to turn aside the needy from justice and to rob the poor
>> of my people of their right,
> that widows may be their spoil, and that they may make
>> the fatherless their prey!

What will you do on the day of punishment,
  in the storm which will come from afar?
To whom will you flee for help,
  and where will you leave your wealth?
Nothing remains but to crouch among the prisoners
  or fall among the slain.

We have lived a long time by the Law. We have prospered when the law of the land in which we lived was most like the ethics of our fathers. When mercy does not prevail and men pursue their own interests without concern for the condition of the poor and the few, when intolerance becomes the rule, Jews suffer. We are few and not powerful; we are important in the world only in that when the few suffer the well-being of all men suffers. Like the Law, the brotherhood of man is immutable; Jews were the first to know; if we are to survive, we must not forget.

Afterword:
On the Separation
of Synagogue and State

America is not Rome; nor is it Jerusalem. We are instructed by Roger Williams and not by Jerry Falwell in God's ability to hear prayers. A Jew may be a Republican or a Democrat, a Democrat may be a Jew or a Christian or an atheist; neither God's Law nor man's law forces a Jew or anyone else in America to choose a political party or a church. The separation of church and state is one of the most basic tenets of liberalism, one with which no reasonable man can quarrel.

Then what shall we do? We were the first ethical religion, and there is no ethics of the next world.

There was no church at Sinai. There was no state. A Covenant was made with the whole man.

Heaven was not promised in the desert. If those who stood before the mountain had immortal souls, no mention was made of it. Earthly creatures entered the forge of the desert and earthly creatures emerged from the desert.

Perhaps it was too long ago. Perhaps we are too old. It has been discovered that Jews suffer genetic diseases unknown to any other people, as if the parchment, knowing too many seasons, has begun to crumble.

The perfection of man is the coming of the Messiah. Perhaps we are too young. It is too soon. We learn so slowly. We die so young.

Slaves left Egypt. A horde gathered at the foot of the mountain. Imagine those six hundred thousand! How many bathed in the desert? How many were hungry? Imagine the sand; how the past disappears in the wind! History in the desert is a day. Who was killed for a cup of water and forgotten in the sand? What was not coveted in the empty desert of Sinai under the killing sun, under the cold stars?

Imagine the stench of them! Imagine the coarse sound of them! Imagine the burnt faces, the dried mouths, the flickering eyes of the wanderers!

What politics were in the desert? The strong survived. The jungle is a gentleness beside the desert.

The desperate people who arrived at the foot of the mountain were no more than a horde. They had known miracles. What miracle left them to wander over the sands of Sinai?

In awe they accepted the Covenant, ethics. They were no longer a horde; civil society was possible. Not in Athens but in the desert, in these poor primitive creatures, was the beginning of political man.

The Law implied an order for man: Ethics precedes politics. The alternative is the horde, in the desert.

When kings were required by war, kings were made, but they were not made holy. David could be a poet but not a priest. And if he had been a priest, it would not have mattered, for priests were not holy. There was God and there

was man, and there was nothing between but the between
itself, the empty space where wisdom might be found.
There was man and there was man, and there was nothing
between but the between itself, the empty space where the
wisdom of ethical life might be found.

A Jew is a whole man in his own time; the Law is now, as
if there were no more days. The lesson of the desert is that
the world exists because of mercy. There can be no civil society without mercy, no peace without mercy. If the Law is
not proof enough, there is also history.

Mercy is the soul and the shield of the Jew. He is an ethical man, therefore a political man. A Jew without mercy is a
man prior to the Covenant; he belongs to the horde; he in-
vites the desert.

Earl Shorris is the author of *The Death of the Great Spirit, Ofay, The Boots of the Virgin, Under the Fifth Sun,* and *The Oppressed Middle.*